SPECIAL MESSAGE TO READERS

THE ULVERSCROFT FOUNDATION
(registered UK charity number 264873)
was established in 1972 to provide funds for
research, diagnosis and treatment of eye diseases.
Examples of major projects funded by
the Ulverscroft Foundation are:-

- The Children's Eye Unit at Moorfields Eye Hospital, London
- The Ulverscroft Children's Eye Unit at Great Ormond Street Hospital for Sick Children
- Funding research into eye diseases and treatment at the Department of Ophthalmology, University of Leicester
- The Ulverscroft Vision Research Group, Institute of Child Health
- Twin operating theatres at the Western Ophthalmic Hospital, London
- The Chair of Ophthalmology at the Royal Australian College of Ophthalmologists

You can help further the work of the Foundation
by making a donation or leaving a legacy.
Every contribution is gratefully received. If you
would like to help support the Foundation or
require further information, please contact:

THE ULVERSCROFT FOUNDATION
The Green, Bradgate Road, Anstey
Leicester LE7 7FU, England
Tel: (0116) 236 4325

website: www.foundation.ulverscroft.com

Jeanette Winterson was born in Manchester in 1959, and was adopted the following year by Pentecostal parents who brought her up in the nearby mill town of Accrington. As a Northern working-class girl she was not encouraged to be clever. There were only six books in the house, including the Bible and *Cruden's Complete Concordance to the Old and New Testaments*. Strangely, one of the other books was Malory's *Morte d'Arthur*, and it was this that kindled her lifelong passion for reading and writing. Winterson graduated from St Catherine's College, Oxford, and moved to London, where she wrote her first novel, *Oranges are Not the Only Fruit*, which won the 1985 Whitbread Prize for a First Novel. This was adapted for television by Winterson in 1990, and won the BAFTA Award for Best Drama. Since then, Winterson has gone on to win numerous awards for her books, and in 2006 received an OBE for her services to British literature. She lives in Gloucestershire and London.

You can discover more about the author at www.jeanettewinterson.com

THE GAP OF TIME

New Bohemia, America. A storm. A black man finds a white baby abandoned in the night. He gathers her up — light as a star — and decides to take her home.

London, England. After the financial crash. Leo Kaiser knows how to make money, but he doesn't know how to manage the jealousy he feels towards his best friend and his wife. Is this newborn baby even his?

New Bohemia. Seventeen years later. A boy and a girl are falling in love — but there's a lot they don't know about who they are and where they come from.

Inspired by Shakespeare's *The Winter's Tale*, this is a contemporary story in which Time itself is a player in a game of high stakes that will either end in tragedy. . . or forgiveness.

JEANETTE WINTERSON

THE GAP OF TIME

TIME

The Winter's Tale retold

HOGARTH
SHAKESPEARE

Complete and Unabridged

CHARNWOOD
Leicester

First published in Great Britain in 2015 by
Hogarth
an imprint of Vintage
London

First Charnwood Edition
published 2016
by arrangement with
Penguin Random House
London

A catalogue record for this book is available
from the British Library.

ISBN 978–1–4448–2893–1

Published by
F. A. Thorpe (Publishing)
Anstey, Leicestershire

Set by Words & Graphics Ltd.
Anstey, Leicestershire
Printed and bound in Great Britain by
T. J. International Ltd., Padstow, Cornwall

This book is printed on acid-free paper

To Ruth Rendell 1930–2015

Past fifty, we learn with surprise and a sense
of suicidal absolution
that what we intended and failed
could never have happened —
and must be done better.

'For Sheridan', Robert Lowell

Contents

THREE

THE ORIGINAL

The Place. The play opens in Sicilia — one of Shakespeare's many fantasy islands.

The Time. Invented.

The Story. Polixenes, King of Bohemia, has been staying with his childhood friend Leontes, King of Sicilia, for the past nine months. Polixenes wants to go home. Leontes tries and fails to persuade him to stay.

Leontes's pregnant wife, Hermione, intervenes, and Polixenes agrees to stay a little longer.

But Leontes believes that Polixenes and Hermione are having an affair and the child she will soon give birth to belongs to Polixenes.

Leontes calls his manservant, Camillo, and orders him to poison Polixenes. Instead, Camillo warns Polixenes that Leontes intends to murder him. Polixenes escapes, taking Camillo with him.

Leontes is enraged at the escape and immediately and publicly accuses his wife of infidelity. He throws her in prison — deaf to the protests of the entire court, especially the noblewoman Paulina, the only person brave enough to stand up to Leontes.

Leontes hates the fact that no one believes his mad, vile denunciations of Hermione, and to avoid being called a tyrant he sends an envoy to consult the Oracle at Delphi.

Meanwhile, Hermione gives birth to a

daughter. Leontes disowns the child as a bastard and decrees her death.

Paulina brings the child in to Leontes, hoping it will soften his rage. Instead he threatens to dash out its brains. Not quite able to face down Paulina, he agrees that the child can be taken to some remote place and cast out to fortune. Paulina's husband, Antigonus, must do the deed.

While Antigonus is gone, Leontes brings Hermione to trial, humiliating her in front of the Royal Court. The more he abuses her, the more dignified she seems, remarkable by her composure, and her steady denial of his madness.

In the middle of this kangaroo court, the Oracle is brought back from Delphi. The Oracle declares that Leontes is a jealous tyrant; that Hermione and Polixenes are innocent; that the baby is innocent and that Leontes will have no heir until the lost child is found.

Leontes flies into a frothing rage and declares the Oracle a lie. As he does so, a messenger runs in to tell him that young Mamilius, his only son, is dead.

Hermione collapses. Leontes repents. It is too late. The Queen is dead.

The Place. Bohemia. Now part of the Czech Republic. It has never had a sea-coast.

The Story. Antigonus leaves the baby Perdita on the shores of Bohemia, with money and some tokens of her birth, and tries to get away before the breaking storm. His ship capsizes. Antigonus is killed in the world's most famous stage direction: *Exit pursued by a bear.*

The local rogue Autolycus notices everything but does nothing, other than pick a pocket or two, as Perdita is found by a poor shepherd and his dimwitted son, Clown. They take pity on the baby and bring her up as their own.

The Time. Sixteen years later.

Prince Florizel, son of Polixenes, has fallen in love with Perdita. He believes she's a shepherd's daughter.

The scene is set at a joyful party — the sheep-shearing festival where our Shepherd and his son, the Clown, are rich, thanks to the money they found wrapped up with Perdita.

Florizel is pretending to be an ordinary guy, not a rich prince. Impulsively he offers to marry Perdita — and asks two older strangers to bear witness.

The strangers turn out to be his father Polixenes and Camillo in disguise.

While Perdita and Florizel declare their love, the rogue Autolycus is busy stealing everyone's money, and lying and entertaining his way through the feast.

He is Shakespeare's most lovable villain — witty, mercurial and uncrushable. And the unlikely means to a happy ending . . .

As the Clown is busy entertaining his lady friends, Mopsa and Dorcas, and the Shepherd is congratulating everyone on their good fortune, Polixenes rips off his disguise and threatens the whole party with instant death.

He storms off, ordering Florizel never to see Perdita again. Camillo realises this is his chance to go home. He offers to take Florizel and Perdita to Sicilia. They agree and escape.

Following behind come the Shepherd, the Clown and Autolycus.

The place. Sicilia.
The time. A fast-moving present.
The story. Florizel and Perdita arrive at Court. Leontes briefly falls for Perdita then discovers she's his own daughter, when the Shepherd and the Clown show up with their box of proof left over from her birth.

Polixenes, tailing the fugitives, is reconciled to both Leontes and Florizel. The end is in sight. Paulina invites everyone to her house to look at a statue of Hermione. This statue is so lifelike that Leontes moves to kiss it, but is warned back by Paulina, who then offers to make the statue step down.

The end of the play, without explanation or warning or psychological interpretation, throws all the characters forward into a new life. What they will make of it is left to 'the gap of time'.

THE COVER VERSION

ONE

Watery Star

I saw the strangest sight tonight.

I was on my way home, the night hot and heavy, the way it gets here this time of year so that your skin is shiny and your shirt is never dry. I'd been playing piano in the bar I play in, and nobody wanted to leave, so I was later than I like to be. My son said he'd come by in the car but he never came.

I was on my way home, maybe two in the morning, a cold bottle of beer heating up in my hand. Not supposed to drink on the streets, I know, but what the hell, after a man's been working nine hours straight, serving shots when the bar's quiet, playing piano when it gets busy. Folks drink more when there's live music, and that's a fact.

I was on my way home when the weather broke in two and the rain came down like ice — it was ice — hailstones the size of golf balls and hard as a ball of elastic. The street had all the heat of the day, of the week, of the month, of the season. When the hail hit the ground, it was like throwing ice cubes into a fat fryer. It was like the weather was coming up from the street instead of down from the sky. I was running through a riddle of low-fire shrapnel, dodging doorway to doorway, couldn't see my feet through the hiss and steam. On the steps of the church I got above the bubbling froth for a minute or two. I was soaked. The money in my pocket was stuck together and my hair was stuck to my head. I wiped the rain out of my eyes. Tears of rain. My wife's been dead a year now. No use in sheltering. Might as well get home.

So I took the short cut. I don't like to take the short cut because of the BabyHatch.

The hospital installed it a year ago. I watched the builders day by day while I was visiting my wife. I saw how they poured the concrete shell, fixed the steel box inside the shell, fitted the seal-shut window, wired the heat and light and the alarm. One of the builders didn't want to do it, thought it was wrong; immoral, I guess. A sign of the times. But the times has so many signs that if we read them all we'd die of heartbreak.

The hatch is safe and warm. Once the baby is inside and the hatch is closed, a bell rings in the hospital and it doesn't take long for a nurse to come down, just long enough for the mother to walk away — there's a street corner right there. She's gone.

I saw it happen once. I ran after her. I called out, 'Lady!' She turned round. She looked at me. There was a second, the kind that holds a whole world — and then the second hand moved on and she was gone.

I went back. The hatch was empty. A few days later my wife died. So I don't walk home that way.

There's a history to the BabyHatches. Isn't there always a history to the story? You think you're living in the present but the past is right behind you like a shadow.

I did some research. In Europe, in the Middle

Ages, whenever that was, they had BabyHatches back then. They called them Foundling Wheels; a round window in a convent or a monastery, and you could pass a baby inside and hope that God would take care of it.

Or you could leave it wrapped up in the woods for the dogs and wolves to raise. Leave it without a name but with something to begin the story.

★   ★   ★

A car skids past me too fast. The water from the gutter douses me like I'm not wet enough already. Asshole. The car pulls up — it's my son, Clo. I get in. He passes me a towel and I wipe my face, grateful and suddenly tired out.

We drive a few blocks with the radio on. The freak-weather report. A supermoon. Giant waves at sea, the river over its banks. Don't travel. Stay indoors. It's not Hurricane Katrina but it's not a night out either. The cars parked either side of the road are halfway up their wheels in water.

Then we see it.

Up ahead there's a black BMW 6 Series smashed full frontal into the wall. The doors are open both sides. Some small junky car is rammed into the back. Two hoods are beating a guy into the ground. My son leans on the horn, drives straight at them, window down, shouting, 'WHAT THE FUCK WHAT THE FUCK!' His car slews in as one of the men fires a shot at us to take out the front tyre. My son spins the wheel, thuds the car into the kerb. The hoods jump in the BMW, scraping it the length of the wall, shunting the junky car across the street. The beaten-up guy is on the ground. He's wearing a good suit. He's maybe sixty. He's bleeding. The blood is washing down his face under the rain. He says something. I kneel next to him. His eyes are open. He's dead.

My son looks at me — I'm his father — what do we do? Then we hear the sirens start up from somewhere far off like another planet.

'Don't touch him,' I say to my son. 'Reverse the car.'

'We should wait for the cops.'

I shake my head.

We bounce the busted tyre back round the corner and drive slowly down the road that passes the hospital. An ambulance is leaving the emergency garage.

'I need to change the wheel.'

'Pull into the hospital lot.'

'We should tell the cops what we saw.'

'He's dead.'

★   ★   ★

My son stops the car and goes to get the gear to change the wheel. For a moment I sit sodden and still on the soaked car seat. The lights of the hospital slice through the windows; I hate this hospital. I sat in the car like this after my wife died. Staring out of the windscreen seeing nothing. The whole day passed and then it was night and nothing had changed because everything had changed.

I get out of the car. My son jacks the back and

together we lift off the wheel. He's already rolled the spare from the trunk. I put my fingers into the ripped rubber of the dead tyre and pull out the bullet. Whatever we need we don't need this. I take it to drop it down a deep drain at the edge of the kerb.

And that's when I see it. The light.

The BabyHatch is lit up.

Somehow, I get a sense this is all connected — the BMW, the junky car, the dead man, the baby.

Because there is a baby.

I walk towards the hatch and my body's in slow motion. The child's asleep, sucking its thumb. No one has come yet. Why has no one come yet?

I realise without realising that I've got the tyre lever in my hand. I move without moving to prise open the hatch. It is easy. I lift out the baby and she's as light as a star.

Abide with me; fast falls the eventide;
The darkness deepens; Lord, with me
*   abide;*
When other helpers fail and comforts flee,
Help of the helpless, oh, abide with me.

The congregation is strong this morning. Around two thousand of us filling the church. The floods didn't put anybody off coming. The pastor says, "*Many waters cannot quench love, neither can floods drown it.*"

That's from the Song of Solomon. We sing what we know.

9

The Church of God's Delivery started in a shack, grew to a house and became a small town. Mostly black. Some whites. Whites find it harder to believe in something to believe in. They get stuck on the specifics, like the seven days of Creation and the Resurrection. I don't worry about any of that. If there is no God I won't be any worse off when I'm dead. Just dead. If there is a God, well, OK, I get what you're saying: so where is this God?

I don't know where God is but I reckon God knows where I am. He got the world's first global app. Find Shep.

That's me. Shep.

I live quietly with my son, Clo. He's twenty. He was born here. His mother came from Canada, her parents came from India. I came here on a slave ship, I guess — OK, not me, but my DNA, still with Africa written in it. Where we are now, New Bohemia, used to be a French colony. Sugar plantations, big colonial homes, beauty and horror all together. The ironwork balustrades the tourists love. The little eighteenth-century buildings painted pink or yellow or blue. The wooden store fronts with their big glass windows curved onto the street. The alleys with dark doorways leading down to the ladies of pleasure.

Then there's the river. Wide as the future used to be. Then there's the music — always a woman singing somewhere, an old man playing the banjo. Maybe just a pair of maracas the girl shakes by the cash register. Maybe a violin that reminds you of your mother. Maybe a tune that makes you want to forget. What is memory anyway but a painful dispute with the past?

I read that the body remakes itself every seven years. Every cell. Even the bones rebuild themselves like coral. Why then do we remember what should be long gone? What's the point of every scar and humiliation? What is the point of remembering the good times when they are gone? I love you. I miss you. You are dead.

'Shep! Shep?' It's the pastor. Yes, thank you, I am all right. Yes, what a night it was last night. God's judgement on the million crimes of mankind. Does the pastor believe that? No, he doesn't. He believes in global warming. God doesn't need to punish us. We can do that for ourselves. That's why we need forgiveness. Human beings don't know about forgiveness. Forgiveness is a word like tiger — there's footage of it and verifiably it exists but few of us have seen it close and wild or known it for what it is.

I can't forgive myself for what I did . . .

One night, late, deep night, the dead of night — they call it that for a reason — I smothered my wife in her hospital bed. She was frail. I am strong. She was on oxygen. I lifted the face cone and put my hands over her mouth and nose, and asked Jesus to come and take her. He did.

The monitor was beeping and I knew they'd be in the room soon. I didn't care what happened to me. But no one came. I had to go and fetch someone — the place had too few nurses and too many patients. They couldn't be sure who to blame — though I am pretty certain they thought it was me. We covered my wife with

11

a sheet, and when eventually the doctor showed up he wrote 'Respiratory Failure'.

I don't regret it but I can't forgive it. I did the right thing but it was wrong.

'You did the wrong thing for the right reason,' the pastor said. But that's where we don't agree. It may sound like we're just tossing the words around here, but there is a big difference. He means it is wrong to take a life but that I did it to end her suffering. I believe it was right to take her life. We were married. We were one flesh. But I did it for the wrong reason and I knew that soon enough. I didn't do it to end my wife's pain; I did it to end my own.

'Stop thinking about it, Shep,' says the pastor.

★　★　★

After church I went home. My son was watching TV. The baby was awake, very quiet, wide eyes on the ceiling where the light made shadow bars through the slatted blinds. I picked her up and let myself out again and headed for the hospital. The baby was warm and easy to carry. Lighter than my son had been when he was born. My wife and I had just moved to New Bohemia. We believed in everything — the world, the future, God, peace and love, and, most of all, each other.

As I walked down the street carrying the baby I fell into a gap of time, where one time and another become the same time. My body straightened, my step lengthened. I was a young man married to a beautiful girl and suddenly we were parents. 'Hold the baby's head,' she said as I carried him, my hand enfolding his life.

That week after he was born, we couldn't get out of bed. We slept and ate with our baby lying between us on his back. We spent the whole week just staring at him. We had made him. With no skills and no training, no college diploma and no science dollars, we had made a human being. What is this crazy, reckless world where we can make human beings?

Don't go.
What's that you say, mister?
I'm sorry, I was daydreaming.
Fine looking baby.
Thank you.

The woman walks on. I find I am standing in the middle of the busy street holding a sleeping baby and talking to myself. But I'm not talking to myself. I am talking to you. Still. Always. *Don't go.*

See what I mean about memory? My wife no longer exists. There is no such person. Her passport has been cancelled. Her bank account is closed. Someone else is wearing her clothes. But my mind is full of her. If she had never lived and my mind was full of her they'd lock me up for being delusional. As it is, I am grieving.

I discover that grief means living with someone who is not there.

Where are you?

Engine roar of a motorcycle. Cars with their windows down and the radio on. Kids on

13

skateboards. A dog barking. The delivery truck unloading. Two women arguing on the sidewalk. Everybody on their cellphone. A guy on a box shouting, EVERYTHING MUST GO.

That's fine by me. Take it all away. The cars, the people, the goods for sale. Strip it back to the dirt under my feet and the sky over my head. Turn off the sound. Blank the picture. Nothing in between us now. Will I. see you walking towards me at the end of the day? The way you did, the way we both did, dead tired, coming home from work? Look up and we see each other, first far away, then near? The energy of you in human form again. The atomic shape of your love.

'It's nothing,' she said, when she knew she was dying.

Nothing? Then the sky is nothing and the earth is nothing and your body is nothing and our lovemaking is nothing . . .

She shook her head. 'Death is the least important thing in my life. What difference will it make? I won't be here.'

'I will be here,' I said.

'That's the cruelty,' she said. 'If I could live my death for you I would.'

'CLOSING-DOWN SALE. EVERYTHING MUST GO.'

It's gone already.

I reached the street where the hospital stands. There's the BabyHatch. Just then the baby I'm carrying wakes up and I feel her move. We look at each other, her unsteady blue eyes finding my dark gaze. She lifts up one tiny hand, small as a flower, and touches the rough stubble of my face.

The cars come and the cars go between me and my crossing the street. The anonymous always-in-motion world. The baby and I stand still, and it's as if she knows that a choice has to be made.

Or does it? The important things happen by chance. Only the rest gets planned.

I walked round the block thinking I'd think about it, but my legs were heading home, and sometimes you have to accept that your heart knows what to do.

★ ★ ★

When I got back my son was watching the TV news. Last night's storm update and personal stories. The usual government officials saying the usual things. Then there was another call for witnesses to come forward. The dead man. The man was Anthony Gonzales, Mexican. Passport found on the body. Robbery. Homicide. Nothing unusual about that in this city except for the weather.

But there was something unusual. He left the baby.

'You don't know that, Dad.'

'I know what I know.'

'We should tell the cops.'

How did I raise a son who trusts the cops? My son trusts everyone. I worry about him. I shake my head. He points at the baby.

'If you're not calling the cops, what are you

15

gonna do with her?'

'Keep her.'

My son looks at me in disbelief and dismay. I can't keep a newborn child. It's illegal. But I don't care about that. Help of the helpless. Can't I be that person?

I have fed her and changed her. I bought what I needed from the store on the way home. If my wife were alive, she'd do what I'm doing. We would do this together.

It's as though I've been given a life for the one I took. That feels like forgiveness to me.

There was an attaché case with the child — like preparing her for a career in business. The case is locked. I tell my son that if we can locate her parents, we'll do that. So we open the case.

Clo's face looks like a bad actor's in a budget sitcom. His eyes bulge. His jaw drops.

'Seven days of Creation,' says Clo. 'Is that stuff real?'

Crisp, packed, stacked notes like a prop from a gangster movie. Fifty bundles. Ten thousand dollars in every bundle.

Underneath the notes there is a soft velvet bag. Diamonds. A necklace. Not little snips of diamonds — big-cut and generous like the heart of a woman. Time so deep and clear in the facets that it's like looking into a crystal ball.

Underneath the diamonds there's a piece of sheet music. Handwritten. The song says 'PERDITA'.

So that's her name. The little lost one.

'You're made for life,' says Clo. 'If you don't go to jail.'

'She's ours, Clo. She's your sister now. I'm her father now.'

'What are you going to do with the money?'

★   ★   ★

We moved to a new neighbourhood where we weren't known. I sold my apartment and I used that money and the cash in the case to buy a piano bar called the Fleece. It was a Mafia place and they needed to get out so they were fine about the cash. No questions. I put the diamonds in a bank box in her name until she turns eighteen.

I played the song and I taught it to her. She was singing before she could talk.

I am learning to be a father and a mother to her. She asks about her mother and I say we don't know. I have always told her the truth — or enough of it. And she is white and we are black so she knows she was found.

The story has to start somewhere.

Spider in the Cup

There was a man lived in an airport.

Leo and his son, Milo, were looking out of the full-length window in Leo's London office towards City Airport and the Thames Estuary. Milo liked to watch the planes taking off. He was nine and he knew all the departure and arrival times off by heart. There was a big chart on the office wall of the routes served by the airport — lines of arterial red like a body-map of the world.

'So is this man a Wanted Man?' asked Leo.

'Nobody wants him,' said Milo. 'He's run away and he's on his own. That's why he lives in the airport.'

Leo explained that a wanted man isn't the same as a man who is wanted. 'It means the police are after him.'

Milo thought about this. He was writing a story for school. The teacher had told them to try and write an opening line that contained all the rest of the story — like in a fairy tale that starts 'A King had Three Sons' or 'There was an Ogre who loved a Princess'.

'He's not a murderer, this man who lives in the airport,' said Milo. 'But he hasn't got a home.'

'Why not?' asked Leo.

'He's poor,' said Milo.

'Maybe he should work harder,' said Leo,

'then instead of living at the airport he could afford to catch a plane. Look — British Airways to New York City via Shannon.'

They watched the plane rise from the runway like an impossible bird.

'When the dinosaurs became extinct,' said Leo, 'they didn't really die, they went into hiding until they could come back as aeroplanes.'

Milo smiled. Leo ruffled his hair. Leo's softness was here, with his son.

'When we die, do we go into hiding until we can come back as something else?' asked Milo.

'Your mother thinks so because she is a Buddhist. You should talk to her about that.'

'But what do you think?' said Milo. 'Look, CityFlyer to Paris.'

'I never think about it,' said Leo. 'Take my advice: don't think about anything you don't have to think about.'

★ ★ ★

Leo had been fired from his bank the year Milo turned four: 2008 was the year of the global crisis and Leo had helped it along, accumulating what his CEO termed 'reckless losses'. Leo thought this was unfair. Everything he did with money was reckless, but no one wanted to fire him for his reckless profits.

As he left the bank for the last time, in his chalk-stripe Hugo Boss suit and Lobb shoes, some anti-capitalist kids demonstrating outside had thrown eggs at him. Leo stood for a moment, looking down at the omelette of his suit. Then he tore off his jacket and grabbed two of the kids, throwing them down onto the pavement. He punched a third against the wall and broke his nose.

Another of the kids was videoing the whole thing and Leo was arrested the next day. His CEO identified him from the footage.

Leo was convicted of common assault, but his lawyer got him off a jail sentence on the grounds of diminished responsibility (being fired) and provocation (eggs). In any case, his victims were unemployed troublemakers. No one seemed to notice that Leo was unemployed too.

It was the unfairness of it all that Leo resented as he paid his fine and court costs. Leo hadn't invented capitalism — his job was to make money inside a system that was about making money. That meant losing money too; the crash was really a game called musical chairs — while the music was playing no one cared that there weren't enough chairs. Who wants to sit down when you can dance? In the past he had lost amounts the size of a small country's GDP but he always had time to get it back and more. When the music stopped he had — temporarily — leveraged all his chairs.

After three months drinking himself into a rehab clinic, and three weeks drying himself out, he had been advised to seek counselling for loss of self-esteem.

For six months twice a week he took a cab from his home in Little Venice to a well-known Eastern European analyst in Hampstead. He hated the soft-clicking door into the therapy room. He hated the kelim sofas and the clock and the box of tissues. He hated the fact — two facts actually, one for each foot — that the analyst wore black socks and brown sandals and kept talking about what he pronounced as AMBI-VAYLENCE.

'You love your mother and you hate her,' said Dr Wartz.

'No,' said Leo. 'I hate her.'

'It is a metter ov the gud brist and the bad brist.'

Leo thought about breasts while the analyst was talking about Melanie Klein. The following week Leo brought a copy of *Nuts* magazine to his session. He gave Dr Wartz a Sharpie and asked him to circle the good breasts and put an X across the bad breasts.

'Objectification of the simultaneously loathed and loved object,' said Dr Wartz.

Leo remembered that Dr Wartz had written an important book called *Objectifying the Object*. He began to drift over a brief History of the Object in History because he was learning that a word has to be used twice over to sound smart.

First there were no objects — just energy. Then after Big Bang or Creation, depending on your point of view, the world itself became an object (a meta-object?) filled with other objects. These needed to be named — the Naming of Objects. Later on, quite a lot of objects were invented: the Invention of Objects. Then, he supposed, with wars and general human idiocy, there was the Destruction of Objects.

24

And there were Objects of Desire. His stomach tightened.

Then he thought of inventories, archives, stock sheets, catalogues, lists, taxonomy: the Index of Objects. There was a book his wife liked, by some American writer, called *The Safety of Objects*. Leo himself knew all about the Status of Objects, by which he meant Objects of Status, like his helicopter (sold). Since quantum theory there was the Oddness of Objects, and, if you were a deep thinker, the Meaning of Objects. And what about the Meaninglessness of Objects?

Yes. When you had so much money that you could buy anything, everything, then you could know what Buddha and Christ knew; that worldly goods were worthless. It entertained him that this knowledge could be got by going in exactly the opposite direction to the great spiritual traditions of the world.

He said, 'Can you ever really know another human being?'

'You cannot separate the observer and the observed,' said Dr Wartz.

★ ★ ★

But you can, thought Leo, back in his office. That is what a surveillance system is for.

★ ★ ★

Soon Leo realised that he did not need to pay £500 a week for two sessions of fifty minutes to understand that he had not been loved as a child. Or that he had filled the emptiness with 'Grosz Gain', as the doctor put it.

'We all self-medicate,' said Leo to Dr Wartz. 'I do it with money. The drinking was a reaction. I'm over it now.'

Leo left therapy, gave up drinking and started his own hedge fund specialising in leveraged brokered buy-outs of businesses that could be asset-stripped and loaded with debt, making a good profit for his investors, and, of course, himself. He called it Sicilia because he liked that it sounded just a little bit Mafia. He was Italian on his mother's side.

Sicilia soon had £600 million of managed funds and Leo was going for the billion. There was nothing better than cash shortages on the ground for making money out of thin air.

★ ★ ★

Back in his office Leo saw that he had confused Milo. Milo was darker and more reflective than his father — more like his mother. Father and son came together over simpler things than life and death. Leo took Milo to football and swimming. He didn't do homework with him or read to him — MiMi did those things.

'Mummy will be here soon,' said Leo, for want of anything better to say.

'Shall I go and write my story?' said Milo.

Leo nodded. 'Take your school bag into the kitchen — get some milk and one chocolate biscuit, OK?'

Milo liked his father's offices. There were

always people to make a fuss of him and things to eat, and best of all there were the planes.

Leo hugged Milo. They loved each other. That was real. Milo was all right again now. 'There was a man lived in an airport,' he said, going out.

Leo turned back to his desk — made by Linley out of long planks of Russian birchwood sanded fine as glass. The office was white space: virgin walls, polar leather sofa, Eskimo carpet. There was a big blown-up black and white photo of his wife on the wall. He kept the digital version as his iPhone screen. The only colour came from a red neon wall sign designed by Tracey Emin.

The neon said 'RISK=VALUE'. It was part of a quote Leo had seen at an OCCUPY demonstration: *What You Risk Reveals What You Value*. The quote had bothered him until he changed it. When he started his new company he had commissioned the neon.

⋆   ⋆   ⋆

Leo leaned forward into his intercom. 'Web-Cameron! I want to talk to you!'

Leo was laughing at his own joke when Cameron closed the door. Cameron was ex-army. He knew how to take an order.

'Cameron. I want you to install a webcam in my wife's bedroom.'

Cameron took this in but he didn't understand it. 'You want a visual surveillance system in your wife's bedroom?'

Leo looked impatient. 'You are in charge of Security and Transport at Sicilia. This is delicate.

I don't want an outsider doing the job. I want the camera to link through here to my personal screen.'

Cameron was uncomfortable. 'I have seen these things on adult viewing sites — but . . . '

'I'm not jacking off on my wife's pixellated tits if that's what you're worrying about. And we're not pimping her for twenty quid every seven minutes to a construction worker on an iPhone with his hand down his trousers. This is marital. This is divorce.'

'You are wanting to divorce your lady wife?'

'Why do you talk like that? Is it because you are Scottish? She's my wife, not my lady wife. I don't have a man wife.'

And then Leo thought of Xeno. And he thought it in a bubble of insight that he burst.

'The truth is, Cameron, that I think MiMi is having an affair. And I want to catch her at it. You know why they call it a webcam?'

'It is a camera linked to the web,' said Cameron slowly.

'It's a spider's web, Cameron, for catching insects. I can't sleep at night because my bed is crawling with insects.'

'Your wife is pregnant,' said Cameron.

'You think the sow can't squeal with pleasure because her belly's swinging with piglets?'

Cameron felt his face go hot. His polka-dot tie was hurting his throat.

'You are speaking of your wife and child.'

'My child? My bastard.' Leo snapped a pencil in half.

'Have you any material reason to believe that

MiMi is having an affair?'

'You mean, have I seen her with anyone? No. Did the private dick who's been trailing her for two months find out anything I don't know already — where she goes, the man she sees, her emails, texts? No.'

'You said you hadn't seen her with anyone.'

'Anyone? No.'

'Then surely this is madness?'

'You calling me crazy, Cameron? You calling me crazy?'

Leo slammed the halves of the pencil onto the desk and came round to Cameron. Cameron squared his feet, relaxed his knees, locked his stomach muscles and stood quite still as Leo walked up to him. Cameron knew how to handle himself. And he knew about Leo's temper. Leo's face was so close that Cameron could see his pores. He was careful not to make eye contact.

Leo stepped back and swung his body to look out of the window.

'Amsterdam,' he said as the plane took off. Then, without turning round, he said, 'She can see the man she's seeing every day of the week and no one thinks about it twice. Except me. I think about it sixty times a minute.'

'I can't follow you, Leo,' said Cameron.

'It's Xeno.'

There was a pause while Cameron took this in.

'Xeno is your closest friend. You are in business with him.'

'Keep your friends close and your enemies closer, Cameron, eh?'

'But you said yourself, you have no grounds for this suspicion.'

Leo turned back into the room. 'It's not just women who have intuition, Cameron. I've known Xeno all my life.'

★ ★ ★

Xeno all my life.

They had met at boarding school at thirteen. Both boys had been sent away by fathers who had gained custody over unfit mothers. Leo's mother had left his father for another woman. Xeno's mother was alcoholic and mentally unstable. The boarding school was neither fashionable nor academic but it allowed their fathers to believe that they were bringing up their sons when in fact their sons were barely at home.

Weekends at the school were quiet because most of the boys went home. Leo and Xeno invented worlds where they could live.

'I'm in a forest,' said Xeno. 'My own cabin. Rabbits come and I shoot them. Bang bang bang.'

'I'm on the moon,' said Leo. 'And it's made of mozzarella.'

'How are you gonna walk on a ball of mozzarella?' asked Xeno.

'Don't have to walk,' said Leo. 'No gravity.'

They listened to David Bowie's 'Space Oddity' and Xeno got into country and western. Sometimes he thought he was Emmylou Harris.

They didn't want to be like the other boys and

30

that was just as well because they weren't like the other boys.

By fifteen they were inseparable. They joined the school shooting club and competed at the target range. Xeno was more accurate because he was calmer. Leo was faster and sometimes won because he fired more shots. They invented a game: GUN BULLET TARGET. Win two rounds and you were the gun. Lose one and you were the bullet. Lose two, and you were the target. Then Xeno added MOVING TARGET and said it made him feel free. Leo didn't understand that. He just wanted to be the gun.

One night after target practice they had sex. It was a cliché. Shower. Hard-on. Three-minute handjob. No kissing. But the next day Leo kissed Xeno in the bike shed. He kissed him and he touched his face. He tried to say something but he didn't know what it was. Xeno didn't say anything. That was like him. Xeno was a bit of a girl anyway, Leo thought. He had grey eyes like a cat and soft, dark hair that fell over his eyes.

Leo was bulkier, tougher, taller, stronger. Built like a rugby player, he moved with confidence but without grace. He liked the watery quality Xeno had.

They went swimming, the sky low, the water warm, gulls patrolling the shoals. Leo was showy and noisy and fast and got tired before Xeno and his long, methodical distance swimming.

Leo waded out of the water, his feet making deep prints on the wet sand. He turned back, hands on his hips, to shout something to Xeno. The sun was in his eyes. He couldn't see his friend and for a second he felt fear.

But there he was, his head and shoulders graceful as a dolphin, swimming back to shore. The image was blurred but it seemed to Leo that Xeno moved like a wave over the water.

Xeno splashed onto the shore. Leo put his arms round him and pulled him down on the sand.

'Do you think about girls when we do it?' said Xeno.

'Yes,' lied Leo.

And then Xeno worried about being gay.

Later, in the dorm room they shared, they lay with their legs wrapped round each other watching *Rebel Without a Cause*. They both wanted to be James Dean but Xeno wanted to sleep with James Dean too.

'James Dean was gay,' said Xeno.

'Was Elvis gay?'

'No, he fucked cheeseburgers.'

'I wouldn't want mayonnaise on my dick.'

'Not even if I sucked it off?'

Leo was instantly hard. He undid his trousers. Xeno knelt down and licked his balls. Leo stroked Xeno's head. Then he started laughing. Xeno looked up.

Leo said, 'I did it with a watermelon when I was a kid. Knifed a hole in the side and fucked it. It was amazing. I was always asking my mum to buy watermelons after that and never eating them. Then one day my mum came in the kitchen and I was standing there with my pants down and this fucking green watermelon stuck on my dick.'

'You twat! Did she kill you?'

'Yeah! She got my dad to give me a lecture on inappropriate objects of desire.'

'Is that me?' said Xeno.

'Don't stop,' said Leo.

★　★　★

Their school was near the coast, and on Saturday afternoons when the other boys had gone home Leo and Xeno took their bikes and cycled down to the cliffs.

One Saturday Leo said, 'Let's see who can cycle the fastest nearest to the edge. Like the car chase in *Rebel*.'

Xeno didn't want to. But Leo was taunting him.

They set off racing. They were both standing on the pedals, pumping as fast as they could go. Leo was on the outside. He hit a rut and slowed. Xeno surged ahead of him. Leo threw himself low over the bike and pushed forward with all his strength. He came level, pulled past, and then cut in. His back wheel grazed Xeno's front tyre.

Xeno fell. The bike separated from his body, turning and turning in slow motion down the cliff.

'XENO!'

There was no reply. Leo saw the bike hit the water.

He remembered the out-of-time feeling of the moment. His heart rate slowing after the race. The sweat on his chest. A gull circling, its lonely cry like his own cry, high-pitched and long.

'XENO!'

Leo cycled back to the school, his strength done, pedalling on fear. He was sick over the caretaker's boots. The caretaker called the police. Leo took them to the cliff path, the police Land Rover radio crackling. The helicopter circling overhead.

Xeno was unconscious on a ledge invisible from the top of the cliff. He had concussion and a broken pelvis but he had fallen into thick heather and by some miracle not rolled over the edge.

The air ambulance lifted him in a sling and took him to hospital, where he remained for the rest of the term.

Leo stopped going to lessons. He walked every day back to the spot on the cliffs.

His father came to talk to him. He made a speech that began, 'I know we've never been close,' and ended with, 'Try to get over it.'

Leo wanted to tell everyone that what had happened to Xeno was his fault. He went to the headmaster's door. He stood outside. He went away again. This happened several times.

At last he was able to visit Xeno in hospital. Xeno looked thin and tired. His torso was in traction. His head was bandaged. He was on a drip. Leo sat in his school uniform by the bed. Xeno took his hand.

And then Leo cried. Silent tears like a close-up in a movie. It was unreal. That this should have happened was unreal. Someone else's life, not his. He had almost killed his best friend.

Xeno came back to school the next year and sat his exams. He did well in maths, computing and English literature and badly in everything else. Leo did badly in everything. It didn't matter. His father had got him an entry-level job with Barclays Wealth Management.

Xeno turned eighteen and bought a camper van with some of the insurance money his father had accepted as an out-of-court settlement from the local authority for failing to maintain safety standards on the cliff path.

Xeno had enough to live on now for a few years. He got a dog from a rescue home, grew a retro ponytail and hit the New Age hippy 'n' rave trail, driving from festival to festival, no mobile phone, few possessions.

He was handsome with a certain vulnerability to him. He soon had more women than he needed. They liked his quiet, brooding face and that he read books and listened to off-grid music, like opera.

Leo, big-boned and Valkyrie-blonde, with his thick, brushed-back hair and a way of talking, looked good in a suit and did well at the bank. He worked sixteen-hour days without complaining, went to the gym at six o'clock every morning and got drunk every night with no effect on his capacity to make a profit. Soon he was getting rich.

He only saw Xeno once in the first three years after they left school. He felt embarrassed by his drifting friend and his lack of success. He offered Xeno money.

Xeno looked at him with those pale grey eyes that Leo had loved and shook his head. He didn't need money. He didn't have much but he had enough for food, fuel, books, the things he wanted to do.

That upset Leo. Everybody needs money. 'Come and stay in the flat for a bit,' he said. 'Have a hot shower. It's November, for Christ's sake. You can't see out of the fucking van for condensation. I'll take a few days off.'

And it was in those few days that Leo discovered his friend was designing computer games.

Leo was playing 'Grand Theft Auto' and shouting at the console when Xeno came in and threw a banana skin at the screen.

'Hey!' said Leo. 'What's with you?'

'Gaming is the best technology mated with prehistoric levels of human development,' said Xeno. 'It's all cars, fights, theft, risk, girls and reward.'

Leo couldn't see the problem. That was his real life exactly. Why should a game be any different?

'Women don't play because it bores them,' said Xeno. 'So that's half your potential market gone. And why shouldn't games be as good as books?'

Leo thought games were better than books. He didn't read. He liked movies and TV and some theatre but a book was too quiet. Reading was so quiet you could hear the pages rustle.

'Relationship-building. Moral challenge,' said Xeno.

'You have to build alliances in games,' said Leo.

'Yeah, but it's instrumental, isn't it? I use you, you use me. In any case, games are too passive. Books change the way people think about the world.'

'Not if they don't read them, they don't,' said Leo.

'Why can't games be a game-changer?' said Xeno. 'Why can't a game make us understand more, see more, feel more? Don't you want to feel something other than adrenalin?'

'Are you gay?' said Leo suddenly.

Xeno shrugged. He had girlfriends but no one special. He hadn't fallen in love but he liked women. He liked real conversations.

Leo hadn't fallen in love either.

They went out for the night. Got drunk. When they came home Leo went into his bedroom and got undressed. He usually watched a bit of porn at night to get to sleep. He called out to Xeno.

'Want to watch some girls with me?'

But Xeno didn't answer.

★　★　★

Cameron left the office. Leo swivelled round to the window. He hated his friend for fucking his wife. Weren't there enough women out there? Everywhere he went, bars, clubs, hotels, boats, there were identical-looking women searching for men. Long hair, long legs, big sunglasses, moulded tits, vast handbag, killer heels. You could rent them for the weekend except that it wasn't called renting, but both parties knew who paid and who put out. You could collect one at the airport with the hire car if you knew what you were doing. He smiled. That would be a good business. Avis, Hertz, Budget. Choose your model. Bodywork. Engine size. Damage limitation.

Men were reluctant to get married — all his friends had put it off till they were at least forty, sometimes fifty. But if they did marry they were reluctant to get divorced. Just a bit of understanding at the airport would make all the difference. A man needs understanding because he is existentially alone. He stares into the darkness.

That was the difference between men and women, Leo thought. Men need groups and gangs and sport and clubs and institutions and women because men know that there is only nothingness and self-doubt. Women were always trying to make a connection, build a relationship. As though one human being could know another. As though one human being could . . . his buzzer buzzed . . . know another.

'Xeno's here,' said Pauline.

'I'm busy,' said Leo.

'I'll send him in,' said Pauline.

★ ★ ★

Men in Leo's position had personal assistants who could moonlight as supermodels in their celery and cottage cheese lunch breaks. Leo had Pauline. When she had started working at his ex-bank she'd been thirty, fluent in three languages with a degree in economics, an MBA, and she had just passed her accountancy exams for fun. She was a much better educated, much better qualified, much better person than Leo, but she was never going to cut it as a trader. Detail was her strength — she could rip through two hundred pages of due diligence in an hour and give him a list of bullet points to fire at the other side. She'd saved him from the worst of a few deals more than a few times. And when he was dumped from the bank she was the only one of his colleagues who went on calling him to see how he was doing. When he had started up on his own he had asked her to come and work for him.

Leo did the deals. Pauline did the detail.

After fifteen years of knowing Leo and the fact that fifteen years had moved her from a sleek thirty to a formidable forty-five, she ran things the way she wanted them to be run and said whatever she wanted to say.

Thanks to Pauline, Sicilia was compliant, transparent, charitable and, if not exactly ethical, they had standards. Leo was OK with that.

Pauline opened the door. 'I said I was busy,' said Leo.

'You're not busy,' said Pauline. 'I'm busy.'

'Bitch,' said Leo.

'Grob,' said Pauline.

'What's a grob?' said Xeno.

Xeno was slimmer than Leo, easy in his creative-tech clothes: black light wool trousers tapered to the ankle, grey lace-up suede brogues and a grey linen shirt that matched his eyes. The shirt had a pink collar and cuffs. He was too well-groomed for a straight guy, Leo thought, and Leo had always assumed there were boys somewhere on the scene.

'I'll get you a Yiddish phrasebook for Christmas — meanwhile use the audio-visual aid standing right in front of you. Hello, Leo. I've met better-behaved apes. Goodbye, Xeno. We'll miss you.'

Pauline stood on tiptoe to give Xeno a kiss.

'You'll see him at the dinner tomorrow, fat-ass,' yelled Leo as Pauline closed the door. 'Is it because she's a Jew or is it because she's a woman?'

'Is what?'

'Is the reason I can't control her.'

'Why would you want to control her? She's great for the business and she's great for you. You need someone who stands up to you.'

'She's trying to bankrupt me. Do you know how much Sicilia gives to charity? Save the Children — we're paying for the whole party tomorrow. Dinner for two hundred donors. Top DJ. MiMi's singing for free, and we're donating £100K.'

'You can afford it. Leo, I came to say goodbye. I'm leaving tonight. I need to get back to NuBo.'

'When did they start calling it that?'

'SoHo, NoBo . . . it was only a matter of time before New Bohemia got it too.'

'Why are you leaving so suddenly?'

'I had a call from the school about Zel. He's not speaking in class again.'

'What's the matter with him?'

'Nobody knows. He's seen a doctor and a shrink.'

40

'A kid of eight doesn't need a shrink.'

'No? We did.'

'We needed parents.'

'That's my point. I'm going home.'

'Where's his mother?'

'She's there — look, I know you find it odd that I had a child with a woman I don't live with or love, but we know what we're doing.'

'So why is Zel not talking?'

'That's pretty low, Leo.'

Leo looked away. He said, 'We have an investors' meeting tomorrow.'

Zeno said, 'There are different ways of doing family. OK?'

'Is it really so easy and civilised?' said Leo.

'Marriage is one option of many,' said Xeno.

'Along with adultery and divorce.'

'What's with you?'

'I'm pissed off with you for dumping the meeting.'

'My son is more important than a meeting.'

'You calling me a bad father?'

'No — you just called me a bad father. Can we stop this? We had horrible families. Every generation gets the chance to do it better.'

'You sound like a mindfulness DVD.'

'And you sound like a workaholic psychopath.'

'At least I'm normal. I'm not gay pretending to be straight or straight pretending to be gay and I don't use my child like a human shield.'

'That's enough!' Xeno picked up his bag and turned to leave. Leo wanted him to leave and he wanted him to stay. It was always the same.

'Xeno! Go if you want to but don't make an

41

excuse. That's all I'm saying. You can never put it like it is, can you? You slide sideways every time.'

Xeno dumped down his bag on the white sofa and turned back to Leo.

'You want to look at the game? I made some changes. Let's take an hour right now and go through it.'

Xeno started unstrapping his bag to get his laptop. Leo went to the fountain and took a long drink of water. 'You put some balls in it? The investors felt like it was love and peace and flower power in la-la land.'

'You don't get points by killing a hooker, it's true.'

Xeno clicked into the game. 'This is not ready and I don't want to be held to it but I've devised something different. It's something I've been thinking about for years, on and off — my Big Game.'

'What you do sells. Stick to it. The soft games don't sell.'

'So I can't experiment because you can't see the ££££ signs?'

'Cut the artist and his philosophy — just show me the game.'

Xeno dropped down a moving screen of cities, their icons recognisable at once — Big Ben, the Eiffel Tower, the Brandenburg Gate, the Harbour Bridge, the Empire State . . .

'You can choose one of nine cities — London, Paris, Rome, Berlin, Barcelona, New York, Hong Kong, Sydney, Shanghai. I'm sick of vertiginous cliffs and cloaks. Dystopian bombed-out landscapes. Trolls. Testosterone. Stolen cars. There are no cars in the game.'

'No cars? Who's buying a game with no cars?'

'The city is occupied by Dark Angels. You can be on the side of the Angels or you can be part of the Resistance. The Angels have two, four or six wings. Some of the wings have eyes. Angels have two dicks.'

'Now you're talking,' said Leo. 'So all the Angels are male?'

'No. But they have a double dick.'

'So who do they fuck?'

'Whoever they can. It makes no difference; they're sterile. Angels are made, not born — like vampires, I guess.'

'And the Resistance?'

'Mortals. Some with special powers depending on what they can win. If you fight with an Angel and win, you get stronger, the Angel weakens.'

'What's the story?'

'The story is this: the most important thing in the world is lost. The Dark Angels don't want you to find it. The only hope for the city is that the Resistance finds it before the Angels do — and destroy it forever.'

'What is it?'

Xeno shrugged. 'You have to find that out too. There are decoys, feints, herrings of every colour including red. But I think it's a baby.'

'A fuckin' baby?'

'It's been done before, I know. That one was called Jesus.'

'I don't get it.'

'Think about all those fairy tales about babies that get swapped or stolen. Think about *The Omen* or *Alien*. The imposter child, the devil child, and the true child who is the saviour. It's like King Arthur or Siegfried — new life. The shining centre.'

'So where is this baby?'

'Growing up somewhere unknown, hidden. You have to find her . . . '

'Why's it a girl?'

'Or him — and make sure you're not bringing home the wrong one. There will be plenty of wrong ones on the way.'

'I think the Resistance should have tanks.'

'I know you do.'

Xeno took Leo into the game. 'This is Paris.'

'That's MiMi's apartment — what are you doing there?'

'It's where it all starts. In the courtyard.'

Leo was sweating. 'Where what starts? Why is it snowing?'

'It isn't snow. It's feathers.'

'What were you doing? Having a pillow fight?'

'It's how the Angels reproduce themselves — but the feathers have to land on water or fire . . . There are different levels in the game, of course. At Level 4 Time becomes a player. Time can stand still, move faster, slow down. But you are playing against Time too. That's what it's called — 'The Gap of Time'.'

'What kind of a title is that?'

★ ★ ★

Leo's buzzer buzzed. It was his wife.

★ ★ ★

MiMi entered the office. Before Leo could get round his desk to kiss her, Xeno was there. Leo saw the way his hand took the small of her back, the way MiMi leaned up towards him. She kissed his cheek and then she put her head in his neck while he hugged her. It was all over in a few seconds.

MiMi went to Leo and kissed his mouth. She was smiling, happy, heavily pregnant. She was on her way to rehearse for the Save the Children dinner. Xeno had texted her to say he was leaving town.

She knew before I did.

MiMi offered to drop Xeno home to pack.

Pop a last ball in the pocket? was what Leo thought, but what he said was . . . 'Tell him to stay till Monday. I've tried, now you try.'

MiMi pushed Xeno down onto the white leather sofa and perched with pregnant difficulty on the edge. She took Xeno's hand, palm upwards.

'Xeno taught me to read palms,' she said to Leo.

I'll bet he did . . . thought Leo; what he said was, 'More New Age bat shit?'

MiMi bent over Xeno's hand, running her finger along the lines. Xeno bent forward with her, his dark hair falling as it always did. His dark hair falling. Leo suddenly felt sick because it was Xeno's body he saw falling away from him.

'You are going on a journey,' said MiMi. 'Across the ocean.'

They were both laughing. They were intimate,

private. Leo, ghost-faced, his beating heart invisible, wondered if he was in the room.

MiMi closed her eyes. '*Mais, je vois un retard. Je vois* . . . that you will be staying in London for the weekend. *Je connais* . . . that a friend of yours is singing, *et voilà!*'

Xeno turned MiMi's palm over. 'I see a beautiful baby,' he said. 'Coming soon.'

★ ★ ★

When they had both left the office with Milo and Leo was alone, he stood in the long glass window watching them all pile into MiMi's pink Fiat 500.

They look like a family, he thought.

He went to the computer and flicked to his wife's Wiki page. There was the photo he had on his wall. She was like a laser of energy.

MiMi

From Wikipedia, the free encyclopedia

Hermione Delannet, better known by her mononym **MiMi** (born November 6, 1977), is a French-American singer, songwriter and actor.

Contents	Birth name	Hermione Delannet
1 Early life	**Born**	November 6, 1977
2 Musical career		(age 39)
3 Personal life		New York, USA
4 Discography	**Genres**	Chanson
	Occupation(s)	Singer, songwriter,
4.1 Albums		actor

Years active	2000-present
Spouse	Leo Kaiser (m. 2003)
Children	I
Labels	Virgin Records, EMI
Associated acts	The Gap of Time
Website	www.mimi-music.com

Early life

MiMi was born in New York, USA, and raised in Paris, France. Her father was a Russian diplomat and the family travelled extensively. Her mother was American and she grew up bilingual in French and English. She performed her first original song, 'Une Femme Abandonée', at the age of sixteen, after her parents separated, and while attending a wedding.[I] In the early 2000s, she developed an interest in bossa nova music. Performing at jazz clubs in Paris, she soon began to attract the attention of record companies. MiMi made her acting debut in 2002 on stage at Théâtre National de Chaillot in Deborah Warner's adaptation of *The PowerBook* — a novel by the British writer Jeanette Winterson.

Musical career

In 2001, MiMi signed a recording contract with Virgin Records. She released her first studio album, *Les Fleurs du Mals*, in 2002 incorporating new wave and bossa nova music.[2] In 2005 she released the album *Rage*. All of the songs on this album are based on solo voice, with a single instrument accompaniment. *Rage* quickly became a gold album. The song 'Dark Angel' is understood to have been inspired by the French poet Gérard de Nerval — who dreamed that an angel fell from heaven and was trapped in a narrow courtyard. Some say it is a reference to her stormy relationship with her husband, Leo Kaiser.

Personal life

MiMi married Leo Kaiser in 2003. The couple lives in the UK.

On April 1, 2004, MiMi gave birth to a son named Milo.

Leo fazed out of MiMi's Wiki entry. *Dark Angel. Dark Angel. Dark Angel.*

New Year's Eve 1999 and Leo was twenty-five and in Paris with a bunch of drunk bankers from BNP Paribas. The six of them had spent 4000[euro] on dinner. Leo hadn't eaten his — somewhere between the courses he had gone out for a kebab and a Coke from one of the vans on the Seine. He sat in his Hugo Boss suit on the stone steps leading down to the river. There was a boy with a tinny guitar singing that song about where do you go to, my lovely, when you're alone in your bed? Leo gave him a 50[euro] note just to make him shut up.

The bells were ringing at Notre Dame. He could hear canon fire a long way off. The year 2000. Wasn't the world supposed to end soon?

Leo finished his kebab and stood pissing against the wall. He felt a hand on his bum. There was a woman behind him, asking for money. How much? Fifty or a hundred. Depending.

They walked without speaking under the arch of the Pont Neuf. In the dark, the woman backed against the wall and got a condom out of her bag. She unfastened her coat and unhooked her breasts from her bra. Leo pumped them while he got hard. The woman hitched up her skirt, squeezing his dick between her thighs for a minute. He liked that. Then she pulled on the condom and slotted him inside her. She wasn't wearing knickers. He was vaguely aware that the only part of him present was his dick. The rest of him was unnecessary, elsewhere. Still, she was warm and tight and she moved well. He came quickly with his face in her neck and his hands on her breasts. She smelled of jasmine.

As soon as he was done she took her wipes out of her bag, gave him one and cleaned herself up, throwing the used tissues into the river. *He had a thought that he would be the father of mermaids.*

He paid her. She kissed him lightly on the cheek and wished him a happy new year, walking away, her heels echoing against the stone.

Leo wanted to call out. To ask her to wait. He didn't know why. Maybe he liked her. Instead he watched her passing out of the darkness, back up the steps. On impulse he followed her.

At the top of the steps he saw her join an older woman, not up for business. There was a sleeping toddler well wrapped-up in a pram. The bus came and the women were gone.

Leo walked unsteadily back to the restaurant. No one seemed to notice he'd been away. They were talking about the Château d'Yquem that to him tasted like golden syrup mixed with mould.

His head was spinning. He wanted to go home.

But the boys were piling into the waiting limo and heading for a jazz club. Leo didn't like jazz. He sat in the small, dark room drinking Mexican beer and playing games on his phone, all through some pretentious, out-of-tune sax solo, refusing to fake it that he understood or liked it.

The wine and oysters at the restaurant followed by the kebab and Coke and beer were making him feel sick. He was miserable and alone, so he talked louder, pushing his chair back, necking the Corona when all he wanted was water and sleep.

Then everybody in the club started clapping and whistling and a small, slight, boyish woman with a face like a pretty sailor in red lipstick, wearing a black dress, holding the microphone like it had something to say to her, started to sing. The piano picked up the tune. The snare drum came in off the beat.

MiMi singing. Her strong, passionate voice — he didn't understand the words, but he was sitting forward as though receiving instruction for a mission he mustn't fail. Leo felt his heart change.

He felt, not thought, Where is this place that I was happy? I must go back there, even if I die.

And he remembered that day on the cliff path before Xeno had fallen.

But you can't reverse time, can you?

Xeno had fallen. Would always have fallen. No matter how close they were, tried to be, had been, from now on fifty feet separated them.

The hospital and Xeno holding his hand. Xeno never blamed him. He never spoke about it to Leo or to anyone. It was Leo who couldn't bear it. Leo who put the distance between them.

No, thought Leo, the distance was there. I didn't know how to close the gap so I made it wider.

MiMi was singing — '*Is that man falling? Or is that man falling in love?*'

And he remembered from school assembly that the Fall is an exile from paradise and that an angel with a flaming sword bars the way.

This is the place I remember, felt Leo. Delight. Certainty. Recognition. Excitement. Protection. Yes.

No sleep on it think about it give me a day or two we'll see maybe I hope so not sure.

Yes Yes Yes Yes Yes.

The fall was when the leaves are shed and Leo felt like he was losing his cover. He felt bare and naked. He felt the wind blowing through him. He felt lighter. She blew through him like a salt wind off the sea. '*I wish you a wave of the sea, that you might ever do nothing but that, move still, still so.*'

★ ★ ★

'I've met someone,' he said to Xeno. 'I'd like you to meet her.'

★ ★ ★

51

Xeno was best man at the wedding. The night before the wedding they went out together, just the two of them, and Leo wanted Xeno to give him away — to be the one handing him over to MiMi. Instead he gave Xeno the ring — because that is what the best man carries for the bridegroom.

Xeno opened the box and took out the diamond. Leo had spent a lot of money. Xeno held the ring to the light. Then he put it on his little finger. Leo was laughing, happy. 'I don't deserve her,' he said.

'Make sure you do,' said Xeno. 'And don't push her too close to the edge.'

Leo wanted to speak. He swallowed, wet his lips. Xeno watched him with the concentration of a cat. Xeno took off the ring, polished it on his shirt and put it back in the box, putting the box in his pocket. He poured them both another drink and kissed Leo, as swiftly as if it had never happened, on the mouth.

Bawdy Planet

Fucking stupid, incompetent bastard!

Cameron had installed the webcam but it had no sound! Leo threw his Himalayan white cushion at the screen. What was he supposed to do? Lip-read?

MiMi was there. Xeno was there. In the bedroom. Together.

Xeno was actually lying on the actual bed. MiMi was not actually lying on the actual bed with him but they had probably had sex already in the oversized bathtub. He needed a camera in the bathroom.

MiMi opened the doors to her dressing room. She said something to Xeno. Leo threw a sweet wrapper at the screen. *He was mainlining Cadbury Mini Eggs.*

WHAT DID YOU JUST SAY, BITCH?

Xeno got up and went into the dressing room. SHIT FUCK!

Leo needed a fucking camera in the dressing fucking room. They were probably doing it on the fucking faux-fur coats like Liberace. Leo needed to webcam the whole house. He needed to webcam her cunt. Then he'd sit inside her and see it coming, that little ramrod dick, circumcised, precise. Leo in her cervix, waiting with his mouth open for Xeno to worm his way in.

Leo pressed ZOOM but the image went fuzzy.

What kind of cheap kit had Cameron bought? Then he saw Xeno's arm round Hermione. No! He was unzipping her dress! Leo froze the image and pressed SAVE. Hard evidence. Ha ha. Xeno was hard for sure. Unzipping his wife.

Leo watched. The dress came off. MiMi walked into the bedroom in her underwear. God, she was lovely. Big tits, slender arms, the bulge of her baby. Bum tight as a wrestler's — Pilates three times a week. Great legs. She wore hold-ups for him. No, she wore hold-ups for Xeno. Leo undid his tie.

Xeno came out holding a dress, his head on one side.

FUCKING FAGGOT WHY DON'T YOU MOUNT HER FROM BEHIND WHERE I CAN SEE YOU?

MiMi was laughing. She used Xeno to steady herself while she climbed into the dress. She's easy with him. You can only be easy like that with someone you've fucked. MiMi got into the dress, wriggled around getting it over her baby, then turned for Xeno to zip it up. He zipped, adjusting her ass-line.

GET YOUR LONG SENSITIVE FINGERS OFF MY WIFE'S ASS!

(He remembered those long, sensitive fingers on his ass.)

MiMi looked in the mirror (DO THEY DO IT IN THE MIRROR?) then looked back at Xeno, who pulled a face and shook his head, making a Marilyn Monroe hourglass shape with his hands and actually wiggling his own faggoty ass like a Thai ladyboy.

WHAT ARE YOU SAYING YOU LITTLE PERVERT?

Hermione nodded and turned her perfect back towards him. Xeno unzipped her. He kissed her neck — it was just a peck but it was a kiss. Then Xeno disappeared into the dressing room and came out with another two dresses, holding them up, one in each hand like a pair of dead rabbits.

MiMi pointed at one of them and the whole pantomime started again. Zips, wiggles, pouts, smiles, laughter, mirror, hair-flicking, head-tossing.

YOU SICK FUCKS YOU CAN'T EVEN FUCK JUST DO IT

Then the bedroom door opened and Pauline came in.

Leo thought he was going to throw up. Pauline! She was in on it. She was protecting them. They were fucking under his nose and Pauline knew it.

DO THEY LET YOU WATCH YOU UGLY BITCH?

Pauline was giving some kind of a printout to Xeno. Again Leo pressed ZOOM. All he got was something that looked like it was written in Arabic.

Here was Leo at work in his office, making money for everyone, and they were in his house having an orgy.

Xeno had his own set of rooms in Leo's house because everyone liked having him around.

YOU BET YOU LIKE HAVING HIM AROUND YOU COCK-SUCKING WHORES

57

Leo had forgotten that Pauline was a partner at Sicilia.

SLAG IN A MARKS AND SPENCER'S TWO-PIECE EVEN THOUGH I GIVE YOU VOUCHERS FOR ANN TAYLOR EVERY CHRISTMAS

He had forgotten that Xeno made enough money to stay in a hotel.

CAN'T AFFORD TO RENT A BED TO FUCK HER IN HAVE TO USE MINE

Leo had forgotten that MiMi earned her own money and owned her own house.

I'LL THROW YOU OUT ON THE STREETS SLUT

They were all pimps and panderers and whores and thieves.

He would kill them.

NOW WHAT?

MiMi was naked. Underwear off. Naked. Pauline sat on the bed chatting to Xeno. What was this? *The Killing of Sister George?* Pauline was a lesbian! That explained it! She couldn't get a man so she had to pimp women. She was a drunk, ugly lesbian. Well, OK, Pauline doesn't drink. Call me a liar over a bottle of whisky. She is a sober, ugly lesbian.

IT'S A THREESOME!

Pauline was about to take off her Marks and Spencer day dress and matching jacket. Underneath would be her Marks and Spencer Big Knickers and wide-strap flowery bra like a hanging basket and maybe a Spanx midriff hold-all whatever. Leo knew about Spanx. He had invested in them. Pauline was going to pull

58

off her thick tights and rub her hundred and fifty tons — OK, pounds — of untoned middle-aged flab over his wife's pussy. Her saggy tits on top of MiMi — was Pauline a Top? All Leo knew about lesbian sex came from porn sites but he was pretty sure there had to be a Top and a Bottom. But MiMi was eight months pregnant — she couldn't have sex on her back. If she couldn't be a Bottom — and she couldn't be a Top because, damn it, she was still his wife — then she must be a Side. Do lesbians have Sides as well as Tops and Bottoms? They must do. He would look it up. His naked wife was about to lie on her side and . . .

Pauline took off her shoes, put her feet up on the bed and started rootling around in her vast handbag — what did women keep in those things? — and then Leo realised: it must be her dildo.

Pauline was getting out an eight-inch purple silicone dildo with a harness. The Big Knickers were coming off. The strap-on was being buckled round her hips, her belly spilling over the top of her moth-eaten German teddy-bear pubic hair, poking out in grey wires underneath.

Pauline was, in fact, still searching through the inscrutable contents of her handbag. She took out her glasses, her iPhone, and . . . a long, red leather object appeared in Pauline's hands.

VIBRATOR THE SIZE OF A SUBMARINE YOU SEX-SHOP SLAG!

It was a pencil case. Pauline settled down to do the *Guardian* crossword.

JEWISH MARXIST!

The bedroom door opened. A pretty woman Leo had never seen in his life before came in holding a zip-up plastic suit-carrier.

GET OUT OF MY FUCKING BEDROOM RENT-GIRL!

Xeno took the suit-carrier from her.

SEX PARTY WITH NURSE UNIFORMS!

Inside the suit-carrier was a sharp-cut blue linen man's suit with a tight white rhinestone V-neck T-shirt. Xeno put the clothes on the bed and started unbuttoning his shirt. Leo had a dry mouth. His friend's boyish, slender chest and back. The scar on the shoulder still visible from where he had fallen. Pauline was looking at Xeno's torso. The tiny gold ring through one nipple. The tiny gold ring in his ear. *Pauline's pelvis was lifting. Her hand was on her crotch, up her skirt. Xeno went towards her and straddled her on the bed. Then MiMi came out of the dressing room and went over to the bed and pressed her body up against Xeno. He turned round and put his tongue down her throat.*

But MiMi was still in the dressing room — and when she reappeared she was fully clothed in a black sleeveless micro-outfit that made her bump look like she was going to give birth to the world.

Xeno put his hand on the bump.

MiMi put her hand over his hand and sat down suddenly on the dressing-table chair. Xeno brought her water.

Pauline got up, said something. MiMi nodded and went to the bed. She lay down. Pauline propped her head up with a pillow.

Xeno came and stood by the bed, his tight crotch on a line with MiMi's head.

SUCK HIS BIG DICK!

MiMi's hand cupped Xeno's bulge. She unzipped Xeno's jeans and let out his cock. He wasn't wearing boxers. She lay on her side, pregnant, towards him, kissing the head of his cock while he stroked her hair. Then she took him in her mouth.

Leo realised he was hard. He stood in front of the screen and unzipped his flies, working in quick, brutal strokes. He sprayed himself over the image of his wife resting on the bed, his best friend standing gently beside her, offering her a glass of water.

Is This Nothing?

MiMi, Xeno and Pauline were on their way to the Roundhouse.

The building had been a tram shed and now it was a theatre and music venue.

Xeno had been persuaded to stay.

'What's got into Leo?' he said as the car moved past London Zoo. 'He's like a bear with a sore ass.'

'He's meshugener,' said Pauline.

'What's meshugener?'

'He's crazy! He's got his own way all his life so he can't control his emotions, desires, rages, affects. He's a typical Alpha Male. They don't grow up, they just get meaner.'

'It's the baby,' said MiMi. 'He didn't want another child.'

'He'll be fine,' said Pauline. 'Leo's got a good heart.'

'He doesn't love me any more.'

Xeno and Pauline looked at MiMi. Then they both started to talk at once.

Ofcoursehelovesyouheworshipsyouhe can'tgeteno-ughofyouyouhavebeenthemakingofhimheknowsthathisli fewouldbe emptywithoutyouareyoufeelingdepressed that'snormalbeforebirthIknowheisn'tthatattentivebuthe watchesyoureverymove.

'I think he's having an affair.'

Xeno and Pauline were silent.

★　★　★

'When I met Leo,' said MiMi, 'he was all swagger and poise. He wanted to impress me with his car, his restaurants, his black American Express after-hours entry to museums and art galleries. He thought I'd like that. We went to the Louvre and the Musée d'Orsay when they were closed. He hired us a private guide. Leo wanted to get up close to the *Mona Lisa* and *L'Origine du monde.*'

'A supermodel and a porn star,' said Xeno. 'That's Leo.'

'He bought postcards of them both and sat looking at them in the car on the way back to his hotel. 'The most famous woman in the world,' he said, 'after the Madonna, but nobody knows what she looks like.' Then he sat with *L'Origine du monde.*

'I said, 'It's just porn. She has no head. No identity.' He became intense. He said, 'It was painted as porn but it explains porn. These two images put together explain why men find women so threatening. The world comes out of your body and . . . ' (he was waving the *Mona Lisa* at me) 'we have no idea what's in your head. Do you know how frightening that is?''

'Leo said that?'

'Yes. And he told me how when his mother left his father, she came to say goodbye and he didn't know why she was leaving, and she said he was too young to understand, and he said, 'I'm a grown man now and I still don't understand.''

'And then?'

'And then he tore the postcards in two and

66

threw them out of the car window.'

'Why did you never tell me this?'

'But why do you think he's having an affair?' said Pauline.

'Leo is possessive but he is afraid of being close to anyone. He would push me away by seeing someone else.'

Or he would just push you . . . thought Xeno, but he didn't say it.

★   ★   ★

MiMi was on stage with the sound guy.

'Xeno!' said Pauline. 'Get over here; I need to talk to you.'

'What's the matter, Pauline?'

'I'm uneasy. There's an old saying — where there's trouble there's more trouble. MiMi's right. Leo's been acting crazy for weeks. Has he said anything to you? About the baby? About MiMi?'

'No. He's just more annoying than usual, but he's my friend so I forget about it. You know me — if there's trouble I go sideways.'

'You think he's seeing someone?'

Xeno shook his head. 'The opposite. I don't think he's seeing anyone; that's the problem. He's blind in his own world — I thought it was about work. He disconnects — right?'

'Yes, he's great at the disconnect. But there's more to this. Xeno — why are you leaving?'

'I have things to do. My son needs me. But, if I am honest, yeah, I feel like I've outstayed my welcome.'

'You're family.'

'You're Jewish.'

'So indulge me and be one big, happy family. It's a fantasy but it's a good one.'

'I have to go Monday latest.'

'MiMi needs a friend. And Leo is pretty unstable.'

'We're all unstable. Leo is like a cartoon of somebody who's unstable, that's all.'

'Leo is like a cartoon of somebody who's unstable who turns out to be himself.'

★   ★   ★

Leo was lying on the white sofa in his white office watching the planes take off. He was thinking of that Superman movie where Lois Lane is dead in her car and Superman reverses time by flying round the earth so fast that he shifts the axis and time goes backwards. The dam doesn't burst. Lois Lane doesn't die.

How can I make MiMi not die?

MiMi's not dead — she's about to give birth.

In my mind she's dead.

Who gives a fuck about your mind?

Me. I need peace of mind.

And Leo was thinking back and back. His bank had relocated him back to England. He had asked MiMi to come with him, to marry him, and she had said no. He left. He didn't call her. She didn't call him.

And then . . .

And then he had asked Xeno to go and find her.

★ ★ ★

Xeno got off the Eurostar at Paris Nord and took
the Metro, line 4, as far as Cité. Then he walked
past the Préfecture de Police and crossed the
Seine. Notre Dame was on his left. The
bookshop, Shakespeare and Company, was just
ahead. He had worked there one summer
— sleeping among the stacks of books on one of
the fleabitten beds.

As he crossed the road he could see the
irascible owner, George Whitman, sitting on an
ancient red moped, and talking to MiMi.

George liked pretty girls. He was in his
eighties now and his daughter was twenty-
something, which told you a lot about George.
And he loved books and writers. Men who
weren't writers usually had a bad time with
George. Xeno had been no exception.

Xeno went over. George scowled. 'Who are
you?'

Xeno held out his hand. 'Hello, Mr Whitman
— it's Xeno. I used to work here . . . I . . . '

'Xeno? What kind of a name is that?' said
George. 'Never heard of you.'

'This is a friend of mine,' said MiMi.

George nodded and started the moped. The
exhaust blasted fumes and smoke round the
tourists.

'Tell your friend to help you mind the store
while I go out for an hour,' said George. 'Don't
lose too much money.'

'Hello, Xeno,' said MiMi. 'Welcome to Paris.'

MiMi went into the store to sit behind the till

that faced the front door. 'I often mind the store for him.'

'Don't people recognise you?'

'They think it's somebody who looks like me. And I do look like me.'

Xeno wandered among the books while MiMi charmed the American tourists into buying two of everything.

'I want to invent a game that's like a bookshop,' said Xeno. 'Layers, levels, poetry as well as plot. A chance to get lost and to find yourself again. Would you work with me on that? I need a woman.'

'Why?'

'You see things differently.'

'I'm not interested in gaming.'

'That's why I need your help. I'll make time circular — like the Mayan calendar; each level of the game will be a time frame — specific but porous, so you may be observed from another level — and you may be aware of another level. It may be that you can operate simultaneously on different levels — I don't know yet. I know it's about what's missing.'

'What's that?'

'You tell me. What's missing?'

MiMi looked sad. She didn't answer. Then she said, 'Is Leo backing you?'

'Yes . . . MiMi, you know why I'm here. Leo loves you.'

'So much so that he didn't call me for a year?'

'Did you call him?'

MiMi was silent.

George returned in a bad temper, carrying a

new cat. Then he told everybody to get out of his store while the cat settled in. Americans and book-lovers alike were bundled onto the streets while George noisily locked the door.

'Isn't this bad for business?' asked Xeno.

'Only time I don't lose money is when we are closed. Then nobody can steal the books.'

SLAM.

MiMi and Xeno were outside the shop. She was laughing. She took his hand.

'All we need now is a lobster,' she said.

'To eat?'

'To walk with us. You know about Gérard de Nerval?'

Xeno didn't.

'You would love him. He is one of my favourite French poets. He had a lobster he kept as a pet and took for walks along the Seine on a leash.'

'What happened to him?'

'The lobster?'

'The poet.'

And Xeno put his arm around her shoulders for a second.

MiMi said, 'It was the nineteenth century. Before Haussman knocked down the slums and alleys and corners of old Paris. It was a medieval city. Gérard de Nerval lived in a building like mine — a seventeenth-century building of small rooms and small windows round a tiny rear courtyard. The square of sky like a lid.

'He had fallen in love with a woman of the lower classes and he was ashamed of himself. One night he had a dream that an angel, vast and

71

majestique, had fallen into the courtyard. Folding his wings as he fell, the angel was trapped. Feathers drifted through the windows into the dark apartments. An old woman began to stuff a pillow.

'If the angel tried to escape by opening his wings, then the buildings would collapse. But if the angel didn't open his wings he would die.

'Some days later Gérard de Nerval hanged himself in the basement from a street grating. A man on the street, walking by, looked down and saw him swinging there, in darkness and alone.'

'That's a terrible story,' said Xeno.

'But what do you do,' said MiMi, 'if to be free you demolish everything around you?'

'But if you don't, you die?' said Xeno.

'Yes. If you don't, you die.'

★   ★   ★

It was August. The banks of the Seine had been transformed into a seaside fantasy, part *plage*, part stalls of street food and pop-up bars. The weather was hot. People were easy.

Xeno said, 'About Leo . . . ' MiMi nodded and squeezed his hand, part reassurance, part understanding.

For a while they walked in silence.

Xeno liked holding hands with women he liked. He liked women. As long as they didn't get too close. And they always did — or thought they did, or tried to. It was easier with men. The sex was simple, often anonymous. A dark stranger whose name (for the night) was love.

Xeno couldn't manage too much nearness. He was solitary and introverted, with an enthusiasm that people mistook for sociability. He was interested in everything, attentive to people, genuinely kind, and entirely present when he was present. But he was never sorry to close the door at night or to be alone.

Leo had sent Xeno to ask MiMi to give him another chance.

'I'll mess it up if I see her. You explain.'

'What do you want me to say?'

'I don't know! The long form of 'I love you'.'

* * *

Leo gave Xeno a piece of paper in his bad handwriting. 'This is the long form.'

Xeno looked at it. He nearly laughed, but his friend was so hangdog and anxious that he just nodded while he was reading.

'I've been working on it,' said Leo.

1. Can I live without you? Yes.
2. Do I want to? No.
3. Do I think about you often? Yes.
4. Do I miss you? Yes.
5. Do I think about you when I am with another woman? Yes.
6. Do I think that you are different to other women? Yes.
7. Do I think that I am different to other men? No.
8. Is it about sex? Yes.

9. Is it only about sex? No.
10. Have I felt like this before? Yes and no.
11. Have I felt like this since you? No.
12. Why do I want to marry you? I hate the idea of you marrying someone else.
13. You are beautiful.

So when they had walked awhile and stopped for water at a bar selling *l'eau* in fancy blue bottles, Xeno got out the piece of paper and gave it to MiMi. She started laughing. 'No, listen,' said Xeno, 'he's awkward but he means it. This is his way of being sure.'

MiMi shook her head. 'I don't know.'

'Then say yes,' said Xeno.

'*Pourquoi?*'

★ ★ ★

They walked on. They talked about life as flow. About nothingness. About illusion. About love as a theory marred by practice. About love as practice marred by theory. They talked about the impossibility of sex. Was sex different for men? With men? What did it feel like to fall in love? To fall out of love?

And why do we *tomber?* To fall?

'There's a theory,' said Xeno, 'the Gnostics started it as a rival to Christianity right back at the start: this world of ours was created Fallen, not by God, who is absent, but by a Lucifer-type figure. Some kind of dark angel. We didn't sin, or fall from grace; it wasn't our fault. We were born this way. Everything we do is falling. Even walking is a kind of controlled falling. But that's not the same as failing. And if we know this — gnosis — the pain is easier to bear.'

'The pain of love?'

'What else is there? Love. Lack of love. Loss of love. I never bought into status and power — even fear of death — as independent drivers. The platform we stand on, or fall from, is love.'

'That is romantic for a man who never commits.'

'I like the idea,' said Xeno. 'But I like the idea of living on the moon too. Sadly, it's 293,000 miles away and has no water.'

'But you have come here to see me because you want me to marry Leo.'

'I'm just the messenger.'

★ ★ ★

They walked to a restaurant in a triangle where some boys were playing boules. A man was exercising two Dalmatians, throwing a red tennis ball. Black and white and red. Black and white and red. The evening was cooling.

They ordered artichokes and haddock. Xeno sat beside MiMi while she talked him through the menu.

'What about you?' MiMi asked Xeno.

'I'm moving to America — the gaming work is there.'

'But you'll be around?'

'I'll always be around.'

What would it be like if we didn't have a body? If we communicated as spirits do? Then I wouldn't notice the smile of you, the curve of you, *the hair that falls into your eyes,* your arms on the table, brown with faint hairs, *the way you hook your boots on the bar of the chair,* that my eyes are grey and yours are green, *that your eyes are grey and mine are green,* that you have a crooked mouth, that you are petite but your legs are long like a sentence I can't finish, *that your hands are sensitive, and the way you sit close to me to read the menu so that I can explain what things are in French,* and I love your accent, the way you speak English, and never before has anyone said ''addock' the way you say it, and it is no longer a smoked fish but a word that sounds like (the word that comes to mind and is dismissed is love). *Do you always leave your top button undone like that? Just one button? So that I can imagine your chest from the animal paw of hair that I can see?* She's not a blonde. No. I think her hair is naturally dark but I like the way she colours it in sections and the way she slips off her shoes under the table. Disconcerting, the way you look at me when we talk. *What were we talking about?*

She ordered a baba au rhum and the waiter brought the St James rum in a bottle and plonked it on the table.

She said, 'Sometimes I'm Hemingway: 11 am a Chamberry kir with oysters. Later, for inspiration, a rum St James. It's a brute.'

Xeno sniffed it. Barbecue fuel. But he poured a shot anyway.

She drank her coffee. A couple walked by

fighting about the dry-cleaning. You meet someone and you can't wait to get your clothes off. A year later and you're fighting about the dry-cleaning. The imperfections are built into the design.

But then, thought Xeno, beauty isn't beauty because it's perfect.

MiMi was sitting with her knees up, bare legs, her eyes like fireflies.

Xeno smiled: what was number 13 on Leo's list? *You are beautiful.*

★   ★   ★

They had finished dinner and were about to walk away from the restaurant, when from a window across the sandy square that was a triangle someone started playing a Jackson Browne number, 'Stay'.

Xeno began to dance. MiMi took both his hands. They were holding each other, smiling, dancing. 'Stay . . . just a little bit longer.'

'Would you like a copy of Gérard de Nerval?' said MiMi. 'I have one *chez moi.*'

★   ★   ★

They walked hand in hand back to the apartment on Saint-Julien le Pauvre.

The staircase was dark. Xeno ran his hand up the seventeenth-century iron banister that curved up the building as the narrow staircase rounded the landings like a recurring dream and the doors were closed onto other rooms.

MiMi opened the door into her apartment. The only light came from the street lamps outside. She hadn't closed the long shutters. She went over to the window, standing framed in the window in her blue dress in the yellow light, like a Matisse cut-out of herself.

Xeno came and stood behind her. He didn't shut the front door and he had such a quiet way of moving that she seemed not to hear him. He wondered what she was thinking.

He was directly behind her now. She smelled of limes and mint. She turned. She turned right into Xeno. Up against him. He put his arms round her and she rested her head on his chest.

For a moment they stood like that, then MiMi took his hand and led him to her bed — a big *bateau lit* in the back of the apartment. She lifted her hand and stroked the nape of his neck.

On the landing outside, the electric light, footsteps up the stairs, a woman's heavy French accent complaining about the hot weather. A man grunting in response. The couple climbed slowly on past MiMi's apartment, carrying their groceries, not even glancing in through the open door.

And then Xeno was walking swiftly down the stairs.

★   ★   ★

It was the night of the concert. The Roundhouse was filling up with guests at the tables.

Leo was wearing a T-shirt that said I AM THE ONE PER CENT.

'Take it off,' said Pauline.

78

Leo took it off. 'You want me to be at the dinner stripped to the waist?'

'Grow up.'

Leo didn't come to dinner. He seemed to disappear. In fact he was in the gallery above the tables and the stage, watching what he had paid for. The evening was going well. The silent auction had already raised over £50,000.

'Where the hell is he?' Pauline asked Xeno.

Leo sat in the shadows, waiting for MiMi to sing. She came on stage, with the quick confidence natural to her. When the applause had died down she made a speech, one hand on her eight-month about-to-be baby, about what it felt like to know that your baby is secure. That your child will have a future. That it is safe to be a mother. Safe to be a child. To give birth without fear. And she spoke as a woman, as the mother of a little boy, as the mother of a new life inside her. The miracle of life. And didn't every woman having a baby want that baby to smile, to grow, to know what love is?

And then she sang. Three songs. They were wild for her. The clapping didn't stop. Some guy in the audience shouted, 'Five grand gets an encore.'

'Asshole,' said Leo up in the gallery. 'You think you can buy my wife for five grand? You can't buy one of her earrings for that.'

Leo looked down. Xeno had his elbows on the table, his face resting in his hands, his eyes on MiMi. She winked at him.

Leo tipped back in his chair. Fell. There was a crash. People looked up. MiMi glanced towards the gallery. She saw Leo. He saw her face, a millisecond register of confusion, anxiety, and, what . . . fear?

But she was singing. She was a pro. She was singing to the end, and taking her applause and smiling. She raised her hand. Touched her belly. She left the stage.

Leo went down from the gallery, backstage, to where the dressing rooms were. He ran down the corridor. 'MiMi!'

She came towards him. She was angry. 'What are you doing? Everybody was looking for you. Why were you up in the gallery? Where have you been?'

Leo didn't answer. He pulled her to him and kissed her roughly. She pushed him. '*Ça suffit!*'

'Stop it?'

'I'm going home. Cameron's at the stage door.'

'I'll come with you.'

'Leo, what's wrong?'

He nearly said, You don't love me any more. She nearly said, There's someone else, isn't there?

Instead she walked past him down the corridor.

Goads Thorns Nettles
Tails of Wasps

One o'clock in the morning.

The streets fuzzy with light rain. The plastic peel-off shine of the pavements. The shimmer under the sodium street lamps. Cars queuing at the red light, wipers in rhythm, drivers with the windows down against the heat. Big guy in a van, his right arm resting on the rolled-down window, elbow out, letting the rain run in, scrubbing his forearm in relief across his face.

Sudden summer rain.

★ ★ ★

Leo watched Xeno putting Pauline in a cab. Then Xeno went towards the underground car park. It was closed now but Sicilia had hired the space. They had the codes. Leo followed him. His own car was down there.

Lower level. Neon-lit. Concrete pillars. Painted bays. Same the world over. Hot like a dry-cleaner's down there, the ventilation shafts whirring to clear the heat.

Xeno could never remember where he left his car. Tonight would be no different.

Leo knew where to find his Jeep. It was one of his fun cars. Ex-army. Khaki body, exposed oversized tyres, canvas top, three pedals, two seats, stripped-out dash with a single speedo dial, big chipped steering wheel, heavy rubber handbrake and a tall, skinny gear stick. He used it off-duty. The Porsche was for work.

Leo fired up the Jeep with the clunky key and turned it 360° on a screeching skid towards level one, where Xeno was backing MiMi's Fiat 500 (pink) out of the parking space.

Leo jammed his foot on the gas, drove full pelt towards the Fiat and rammed it from the rear. Xeno stalled. What the . . . ? By the time he recognised the Jeep and realised it was Leo, Leo was reversing fast down the arrowed one-way he had just driven up the wrong way. His Jeep disappeared round the corner, revs high, the engine noise bouncing round the concrete.

He's on something, thought Xeno, looking at the caved-in flank, pink flakes of paint floating like fish food in the shallow puddles on the concrete floor.

Xeno got back into the car and drove. The wheel was catching where the wheel arch was dented. Better try and pull it free.

Xeno got out, leaving the engine running, and went round to the rear. He pulled at the dented arch.

There was a scream of rubber like a bad movie. Xeno looked up as Leo came racing towards him, leaning out of the low door of the Jeep.

HERE'S WHAT YOUR GAME NEEDS

Xeno jumped sideways. Leo smashed into the Fiat.

'You crazy fuck!' shouted Xeno, but Leo was disentangling the bull bar on the front of the Jeep from the rear of the defeated Fiat by a series of thrusts and dives — and seemed not to notice Xeno any more. Xeno stood back as Leo, once loose from his prey, drove straight into the car again — this time taking out the passenger door.

Something snapped in Xeno. He got back into what was left of the Fiat and turned on the engine. It fired. He headed for the exit signs.

Leo was coming after him.

Xeno ramped the Fiat up to level two, spinning the wheel as he cut crazily towards the exit. Leo was faster and right behind him. He shunted the Fiat, throwing Xeno and the car sideways. Xeno saw a space — too small for the Jeep — and swivelled left, leaving Leo jolting back into reverse.

But the turning Xeno had taken was a mistake. He was driving downwards, not upwards. He was driving deeper into the underground car park.

And Leo was still coming after him.

Head-on.

Somehow Leo had got in front of Xeno. The Jeep took a concrete corner on two wheels and pounded towards the Fiat. Xeno did the only thing he could do and spun the car to avoid the head-on collision Leo wanted.

The impact shattered the windscreen and knocked Xeno halfway out of the open passenger side of the Fiat. He was dazed for a moment, hearing acutely the distressed whine of the car's instrument panel — seeing the yellow and red lights flashing their end-of-the-world warnings across the dials.

He had to get out. Go!

Xeno slid across the seats and pushed open the crippled driver's door. He started to run.

And Leo came after him in the Jeep.

He's trying to kill me.

Xeno was running. He was fast but the Jeep was faster. The neon overheads blurred. Numbered bays — 20, 21, 22, 23, 24, 25. A metal screen ahead. The Jeep was right behind him, Leo's fist on the horn. Xeno could feel the heat from the engine. Leo was going to crush him against the barrier.

Xeno threw himself forward, hit the top of the barrier and vaulted over. As he dropped heavily and painfully down the other side, Leo rammed it. Xeno heard the clunk of the reverse gear as he lay on the floor, the cold metal against his back. Then Leo hit the barrier again. And again.

Xeno was on his feet. He could feel damp air on his face. He must be nearly out. Yes. There was the yellow barrier. He ran out onto the street. He still had his phone.

'Cameron? I need my bags from the house. Especially I need the briefcase — red leather, on the desk — and the laptop. I'll be at Pauline's.'

Cameron was in his pyjamas. 'What's the problem, Xeno?'

'Leo is trying to kill me.'

★ ★ ★

Cameron dressed quickly and drove from his flat in Ladbroke Grove back to the house in Little Venice. Why had he put the webcam in MiMi's bedroom? Why had he not refused to do it?

He entered his code, drove through the gate and saw the light on in MiMi's bedroom. The rest of the house was dark.

Cameron pulled his car out of view of the road and walked down the side of the house to the little guest annexe where Xeno always stayed. The luggage was already packed. Cameron threw the last of the things into a holdall, took the briefcase and laptop, and went back towards his car. Sound of tyres/streaks of light under the heavy metal entrance gates alerted him to Leo's Jeep pulling up outside.

Cameron took out his iPhone and disabled the entry code.

He switched to screen mode and watched Leo through the camera on the gate. He was jabbing the buttons. If he tried the housekeeper or MiMi they wouldn't be able to open the gates either. But then Cameron's phone rang.

'Leo?'

The fucking fuckers fucked

It crossed Cameron's mind that this was a perfectly good sentence — adjective, noun, verb. Not Shakespeare certainly, but adequate.

After a moment's negotiation Leo agreed to drive round to Cameron's flat to get the override key. Cameron watched the headlights fade and disappear, then he opened the gates and left, carefully resetting the entry code.

Cameron drove north to Pauline's house in Belsize Park. The lights were on downstairs and Pauline opened the door in her Marks and Spencer dressing gown. She liked Marks and Spencer.

'What the hell is going on?' said Pauline. 'I'm having a Scotch and I don't even drink.'

Cameron's phone rang. *Leo*, he mouthed to Pauline.

There was a long, shouting rant at the other end of the phone that ended in Cameron telling Leo he had misunderstood. Cameron had been to the house and reset the codes. Yes, Leo could go home.

The phone went dead.

Xeno came downstairs in another of Pauline's fleecy dressing gowns. He had had a shower. His legs were bruised and he had a cut on his face where the windscreen had shattered. He opened his bags to find clean clothes.

'You should go to the hospital,' said Pauline.

'No hospital, no police,' said Xeno, 'but Cameron, you have to get what's left of MiMi's Fiat out of the car park. She doesn't need this.'

'Why was Leo chasing you round the car park?' asked Cameron, though his heart was heavy because he knew why.

'Murder.'

Pauline shook her head. 'That's melodramatic.'

'Do you want to come and see what's left of the melodramatic car?'

'We can tow it out with the Range Rover,' said Cameron.

★   ★   ★

Leo was back at his house. He liked his house. An 1840s white stucco villa with gardens back

88

and front. Private and secure. He had bought it when he had married MiMi in 2003. He had just finished paying for it when he had lost his job. For a year things had been difficult financially — in fact, they hadn't been difficult because MiMi had paid all their living costs. Leo hated that. It made him feel worse than being in debt. He was proud of his wife. Proud that she earned real money. But in his head it had to be all him. If he thought about it he knew it was unreasonable and so he did what he always did and didn't think about it.

But now Leo was thinking about something he didn't want to think about and he couldn't stop thinking about it.

His wife and his baby weren't his wife and his baby. He knew it with every fibre of his being. What a cliché.

★   ★   ★

Leo pulled into the drive and parked the Jeep in the garage. He was calm now. He looked normal. He walked straight to the annexe.

He wanted Xeno's briefcase and laptop. He put on the light. Why was the room empty? He had spoken to Xeno in here just before he had left for the charity event. Leo went into the bedroom, opened the cupboards, then the bathroom door. Xeno had checked out as neatly as if it were a hotel.

★   ★   ★

Pauline was sweeping up the glass round the smashed-up Fiat while Cameron and Xeno hooked it onto the tow bar of the Range Rover.

'He doesn't normally do drugs,' said Xeno. 'He must have started at the party and got off his head.'

'But why would he do that?' said Pauline. 'He's been clean for years.'

Cameron looked at Xeno. 'He thinks you're having an affair with MiMi.'

Xeno and Pauline stood still like animals who've heard the hunter.

'He told me so himself.'

Xeno stood up. His face looked gaunt under the harsh low neon.

'I'm not having an affair with MiMi.'

'MiMi,' said Pauline. 'Gevalt, where is she?'

'At home, of course,' said Cameron. 'I took her myself. Why? Where are you going?'

⋆   ⋆   ⋆

Leo threw the table lamp across the room. It broke against the wall. Xeno knew he knew. Knew he knew what he knew. And he had got away. Someone had helped him. That was why MiMi had been in a hurry to be gone.

Leo went towards the house.

⋆   ⋆   ⋆

MiMi was sleeping.

Leo opened the bedroom door. He had taken off his shoes. Now he took off his jacket.

MiMi always slept with a night-light, a low, soft, child's rectangle of moonlight. And she liked the curtains open. Leo could see her clearly, one arm across the pillow, her body curled on its side in a white kaftan.

Leo stood over the bed. He loved her so much. His feelings were a mixture of tenderness and pleasure and wonderment that she loved him. There was nothing he wouldn't do for her. He kept cuttings of all her press notices. It was him, not her, who had the awards lined up in his study at home.

And she was so tiny, a bird of a woman — no, she wasn't a bird because she had muscle — she was a flower — but she wasn't a flower because she wasn't for display — she was a jewel — but she wasn't a jewel because he couldn't buy her.

He sat on the edge of the bed, watching her sleeping, his mind moving over the past, or perhaps it was the past moving over his mind.

Do you remember when Milo was a little boy and you were singing in Sydney and we went up to Byron Bay for the weekend and we were swimming near the lighthouse and there was a rip tide? I lost sight of you. I thought you had drowned. All that was in my head was that I would never see you again. It was all I could do with all my strength to get back to the beach. I crawled through the surf, my lungs half-full of water, and when I looked up you were there — as miraculous as a mermaid. I would have given my life to see you safe — and you were safe.

Leo sat on the edge of the bed, taking off his socks. He knelt across MiMi's sleeping body. Wake up, wake up, wake up, MiMi, wake up.

★ ★ ★

MiMi opened her eyes. Leo?

Leo was pulling his shirt over his head. MiMi lifted her hand and touched his chest. He grabbed her hand like he was steadying himself from falling.

'Too hard,' said MiMi, but Leo held her harder. He bent low over her, sliding his body flat, his other hand on her throat.

For a second she thought it was a game and then she knew it was not.

'LEO!'

'Did you sleep with him before the show or did you have a quickie when you came back and helped him pack?'

'Leo, *laiche-moi!*'

Leo had unzipped his trousers. He needed both hands to get them off. MiMi moved to get out of bed. He pulled her down.

'How long have you been having an affair with Xeno?'

He saw her face. Disbelief. They never thought he'd find out.

'You cheap slut.'

Leo had MiMi on her side, one hand over her mouth. She was biting him like a dog. She was a dog. He tried to get his penis inside her from behind but she was struggling. He didn't want to hit her.

Leo got up, forced her legs open with his knee. '*I know all about you*,' he said.

MiMi suddenly stopped struggling. She turned on her back, panting, one hand on her belly.

You know nothing about me.

Leo was low over her body, his weight on his arms either side of her. His face close to hers. He wanted to kiss her. He wanted to cry.

'You're mine. Say you're mine.'

MiMi said nothing.

'How does he touch you? Does he lie next to you? On top of you? Does he do oriental massage? Does he rub your temples? Does he go down on you like I do? Do you like that? Do you like it?'

Leo shook her. She was floppy like a just-dead person. She didn't move under him the way he liked, she didn't whisper to him in French; he loved that. She lay still like an animal being beaten. He couldn't come. He kept pumping but he couldn't come.

He leaned to kiss her. She bit his top lip. He felt the blood running into his mouth. BITCH. He hit her across the face.

That's when he saw the car headlights sweep over the wall above the bed.

He jumped up, looked out of the window. Pauline's Audi meant Pauline. Yes. The front doorbell started going like a fire alarm.

Leo grabbed his trousers and left the bedroom, ran downstairs zipping his fly. A door opened on the landing. It was Milo in his Superman pyjamas. 'Daddy? Where's Mummy?'

'She's in the bedroom. Go back to bed. It's only Pauline.'

Milo moved to the top of the stairs as Leo opened the door. Leo tried to look calm —

'Pauline! Are you all right?'

Pauline pushed past him into the hall. He noticed her cardigan was buttoned up wrong.

'Where's MiMi?'

'She's asleep. We were all asleep.'

Pauline glanced up the stairs and saw Milo. She smiled and waved at him. He waved back. Pauline hesitated. 'Is everything all right?'

'Sure, sure,' said Leo. 'Let's all get some sleep, shall we?'

Pauline looked at Leo. She knew he was lying.

There was a crash upstairs. Milo ran along the landing. 'MUMMY!'

Leo bounded up the stairs, Pauline coming after him. MiMi was on the floor, panting, a red weal across her face. Milo was kneeling next to her.

'Bébé,' said MiMi, trying to reassure her son.

'Her waters have broken,' said Pauline. 'Leo! Help me to get her on the bed and phone an ambulance. It's all right, Milo — Mummy's having a baby, that's all.'

Leo scooped up MiMi and carried her easily into the bedroom. He put her on the bed. She was breathing heavily through her mouth. Pauline took her pulse.

'Get hot water and towels.'

Leo went into the bathroom. Milo was standing like a statue in the doorway. Pauline went to hug him. He was small for his age.

'Milo! Don't be frightened. This is how you were born — it's how everyone is born. Go back to bed and have a little slufki. Daddy will come soon.'

MiMi held out her hand to Milo. The boy ran forward and put his hand in hers, pressing his body against the bed, as Leo came out of the bathroom with a stainless-steel bucket of water and all the towels.

'Take Milo,' said Pauline. 'And call the doctor.'

Leo nodded. MiMi didn't look at him. When he had gone she held out her arms to Pauline.

'It's now,' she said, getting off the bed and kneeling on all fours, rocking slightly.

'Just wait for the doctor,' said Pauline.

★   ★   ★

The baby came so fast that Pauline didn't have time to panic. She was kneeling by MiMi as she saw the baby's head appear, then the little red body, legs, tiny feet. She caught the child and laid it on the towels. Scissors; she needed scissors. 'Dressing table,' said MiMi. Pauline cut the cord and took up the baby.

'It's a girl,' said Pauline, and there was a cry like life — it was life — raw and bloody and new. Pauline gave MiMi her baby and the two women sat smiling at each other, not saying anything, amazed in the presence of something as impossible and ordinary as a baby.

Pauline gently wiped the baby's head and face with warm water.

95

The door opened. It was Milo.

'Come and meet your little sister,' said MiMi. 'Don't be frightened.'

'Aren't you supposed to have babies in hospital?' asked Milo.

'She came early,' said Pauline. 'Look, here she is.'

'Where's Leo?'

'Daddy's sitting on the stairs,' said Milo. 'Did I look like that?'

Pauline went out to find Leo. She could see him at the bottom of the stairs as she turned round the landing. He had his head in his hands.

'Mazeltov,' said Pauline, putting her arm round him as she came beside him. 'What did the doctor say?'

Leo shrugged her off. 'I didn't call the doctor.'

'What?'

'Xeno can call the doctor. It's his child.'

Pauline didn't answer. She got up and went down to her handbag on the hall table. She started rootling around for her phone. Leo watched her a moment then turned and ran up the stairs.

'LEO!'

Pauline had to think. She had to call someone. Her phone wasn't in her bag — had she left it at home? It was the middle of the night. Maybe it was in the car. She went to the office Leo kept at the front of the house; the door was locked. She could feel her heart over-beating. She went across the hall to the big, wide living room — there was a phone in there. She put on the light — saw the phone — pressed the call key.

Nothing. And again. Nothing. What was going on?

The kitchen — there was a phone on the wall. Pauline ran — she wasn't good at running — into the basement kitchen; the low counter lights were still on. The remains of a sandwich by the bread bin. There was the phone. She punched in 999. Dead.

The house had a four-line switchboard for Leo, MiMi and their assistants. Leo must have disabled the system.

★　★　★

Leo was sitting cross-legged opposite MiMi. His feet were bare. He hadn't put on a shirt. He looked like a husband who had been with his wife through the birth of their child.

MiMi was watching him the way you watch a dog that will spring. She was holding her baby against her, wrapped in a towel. Small noises came from the towel but Leo couldn't see the baby.

'How long has it been going on? Nine months, yes — but before that? Years? Did you ever really marry me?'

MiMi didn't answer.

'The way you lift your face to him, the way you hold his hand, you giggle with him. Do you think I'm stupid? OK, I am stupid — not artsy like you two — I don't read, don't go to the opera, can't play the piano; I'm no match for either of you, am I?'

'I think I'm bleeding, Leo. Will you get a doctor?'

97

'Just tell me the truth.'

MiMi was still trying to clear the afterbirth. She lay back, legs open, pushing out the placenta. Leo felt ridiculous; his head hurt. There was his wife. There was a baby. What was the matter with him? MiMi was struggling. What if she died?

* * *

Downstairs Pauline found that she couldn't get out of the house. The doors and windows were locked. She had tried every exit, every might-be-an-exit. She was back in the kitchen when Milo appeared in his pyjamas holding his Superman bear.

'Mummy's crying.'

* * *

In the bedroom the red, liverish afterbirth lay on the towel. MiMi was curled up on the carpet, very still, with her baby. The baby was sleeping. MiMi could feel her heartbeat. It seemed steady enough and she was warm. She's strong, thought MiMi.

'I should call Xeno,' said Leo. 'Tell him to come and look at his kid. But I don't know where in the world he is — shall I call him? Let's call him. Do you want to talk to him? Yes you do you do you do.' Leo pushed his foot into MiMi's back. Not hard but not soft either. He found his phone in his jacket. Speed-dialled Xeno. It went straight to answerphone . . . 'Hi, this is Xeno . . . '

Leo killed the phone, mimicking the message. 'Hi, this is Xeno . . . You know he's gay, don't you? He's so self-hating he has to fuck his best friend's wife to feel like a man.'

'He doesn't fuck me,' said MiMi.

'What's that?' said Leo, raising his voice. 'What's that?' He shook her shoulder. She pulled her body away. He crouched over her. 'The father doesn't want to see his baby. The father leaves his bastard behind for his friend.'

'You're sick,' said MiMi. 'No child is a bastard.'

'My language offends you? Well, your behaviour offends me.'

'Call the doctor, Leo.'

★ ★ ★

In the kitchen Pauline wrapped Milo in a throw and put him on the sofa with an iPad. She heated him some milk and told him not to worry. Then she had a thought. 'Have you got your own phone, Milo?'

'Yes, but just for texts — it's in my school bag in my room. Why?'

Pauline crept upstairs. Milo had left his door open. She found the phone. Cameron's number was in there. COME TO LEO'S. AMBU-LANCE ASAP.

★ ★ ★

MiMi was sitting up now. Leo was silent and still.

'I know you didn't want this baby.'

'I don't want Xeno's baby.'

'She's yours. Do you want to see her?'

MiMi unwrapped the child and leaned forward to Leo. He was trembling. He couldn't lift his head. He couldn't look up. His body was not his.

★ ★ ★

When the ambulance came, Leo unlocked the door and let them in without a word. Cameron was behind them.

'I've towed the Fiat.'

'I suppose you towed Xeno too?'

'He's gone.'

'Coward.'

'What's got into you, Leo?'

'You want to see some evidence? Come in here.'

Leo pushed Cameron into the office and put the webcam footage on his screen. The men watched in silence. Neither of them heard Pauline come in behind them.

'Is that it?' said Cameron.

'Obviously that's it — what more do you need?'

'If MiMi has any sense she'll divorce you,' said Pauline.

Leo turned round — his body was slight-shaking like he was caught in an electric fence. 'Divorce me? I'm taking this to my lawyer tomorrow.'

'Why? You want to make him laugh?'

100

'You've known from the beginning, haven't you?'

'Known what? That you can't hold on to anything good? That you only know how to self-destruct? You've lost your wife and your closest friend on one night. Well done!'

'Get out, you interfering bitch.'

'I'm going,' said Pauline. 'I'm going to the hospital with MiMi. Who's going to look after Milo?'

'Milo's my son. I'll take care of him.'

'He's your son,' said Pauline. 'And you have a daughter, Leo.'

* * *

The house was quiet. Leo didn't know what time it was or how many hours had passed since the night started. It seemed like it had been night forever. He wondered if it was possible for night to follow night without daytime, without sun.

He was still in his trousers, no shirt. He was cold, but it wasn't a feeling, more a knowing, because his skin was white and bumpy. He couldn't feel anything. Why wasn't it dawn yet?

He went down into the kitchen. Someone had been heating milk — there was milk in the pan. Leo picked it up and drank what was left, not caring that it spilled down his chin onto his chest. Then he saw Milo, curled up on the sofa, sleeping deeply. He wondered if it was Milo, or a copy of Milo — or maybe it was Leo that was the copy of himself. Things looked the same but nothing was the same — not now.

Milo's iPad was still running. Leo bent to turn it off. *Superman: The Movie*. 1978. It was their favourite. Leo flicked back to the scene he loved — Superman reversing time. Lois Lane doesn't die.

Her car's stalled in the canyon. She turns the engine over and over. Above her the dam is breaking. The rocks are coming down the cliff face. It's too late.

Light belts the globe three times a second. Can I not do the same?

Take us back to a time where none of this has happened.

There's the world hanging in space. There's Superman beating the speed of light — turning all his love into speed and light — and forcing time to defeat itself. He's spinning the world so that the water is pulling back into the dam and the rocks are anchoring their rockness back into the cliff face. Slowly the red car rises from the ravine, the metal body undents, the windscreen unshatters. She's turning over the engine again. It's not too late.

But you can't reverse time, can you?

★ ★ ★

Leo went and picked up his son, who snuggled sleepily against him. Leo felt his breath on his neck. He had carried him like this when he had been a baby. He loved him uncomplicatedly. He never wondered about it or worried about it. It was love as regular as breathing.

Leo carried them both through the shadows of

the house. He was carrying Milo and he was carrying himself. He had to hold himself together. He had to remember what was happening. The party. The car park. Xeno. MiMi. When was all that? It felt like a long time ago. There was no one here. It must have happened a long time ago.

Milo's door was open. Leo went inside and pushed the door shut with his body. The night-light was on, casting its moonbeams across the wall.

Leo laid Milo down in the rucked-up bed. He was suddenly tired. So tired. He eased Milo gently over to the wall and got in beside him, pulling the covers up over them both. His son put his arm across his father's chest. The small, determined warmth of him was like sleep. It was sleep. Leo began to drift away, his eyes closing, his breath slowing.

When he woke up it wouldn't be night. When he woke up it would be different.

Don't be afraid.

My Life Stands in the Level of Your Dreams

MiMi was lying in the hospital bed, looking at the ceiling.

She knew she had to keep still. If she moved her wings she would topple the houses into the street. But the houses had toppled, hadn't they?

How had the angel fallen into the courtyard? That hadn't been explained — the sudden drop, the sudden folding of wings to stop them breaking.

And was the angel alone in the courtyard?

They had given her an injection to make her sleepy. An opiate of some kind. She was part dream, part one who dreams.

It is never fully dark in a hospital room. Never quiet. She heard the call bell from the room next door and the nurse coming down the corridor. The baby was breathing quietly.

She wanted to adjust her pillow.

What had happened to the cushion stuffed with the angel's feathers?

The door opened. The nurse deftly fastened the wide band round MiMi's upper arm and took the blood-pressure reading. The machine beeped.

'Do you believe in angels?' said MiMi.

The nurse was African. She belonged to an evangelical church. 'Let me show you some-thing,' she said. She pulled back the curtains. MiMi could see the old church outside the window. 'Look up high,' said the nurse. The church had a clock tower. On top of the tower, one at each compass point, were four stone angels. 'You see?' said the nurse. 'How they see it all? The cars going by, the men and women on the streets. All the hope and the heartbreak. Yes, that is what they see. And though the earth is lost, she will be found.

'Whatever is lost will be found.'

Feathers for Each Wind

Leo was talking to his gardener, Tony Gonzales.

'Fifty large, Tony; you can retire. All you have to do is take the baby to Xeno.'

£50,000 is a lot of money.

Leo was persuasive. He had the story all worked out. Start again. He couldn't raise another man's child, not when it was his best friend — his best man at his wedding — who had betrayed him. MiMi was ill, guilty, distracted. She didn't know what to do next. Surely Tony could understand that? Yes, Leo said he had spoken to Xeno. Yes, Leo said Xeno had agreed to take the child.

But still Tony looked puzzled. It was all moving too fast. He was a gardener. Nature takes time.

'So why does he not come himself?'

'Tony, Tony, how would you feel in my situation? I never want to see Xeno again. And I never want MiMi to see him again. Understand?'

Tony understood. He was sixty-two. His parents had come to England from Mexico in the 1950s. They had eloped together in Xalapa — her from a convent school, his father from the military. His father had found work slum-clearing for housing in the East End of London. He had been killed on a building site when Tony was two. Soon after, too soon after, his mother married the foreman of the site — and Tony

111

always believed that man had killed his father; there are many ways of killing someone — a block of concrete falling from a crane is just one.

There were more children. Tony was neglected. Then beaten. His stepfather didn't want him. His mother couldn't protect him. The blues and yellows in her Xalapa soul had dirtied down to English grey. She was indifferent, then depressed. Tony had left home at sixteen, slept in a hostel and got a low-paid job sweeping leaves in the royal parks. But he loved plants and he soon learned. He studied for a horticulture degree at the Open University. He never married. He didn't trust human nature. Plants were better. When he retired from the parks at sixty, as a senior gardener, he had taken a part-time job with Leo and Sicilia.

He managed the garden in Little Venice and the planting and landscaping at the offices. Lately, he had been working for Pauline too. He liked Pauline. When he worked in her garden he tied up a bouquet of stems, leaves, flowers, whatever was in season, and left it in water in the watering can by the back door. She made him think — almost — that . . . perhaps.

And Pauline liked Tony. He was built like a small bear. Strong arms. Hands that were never quite clean. He always wore a tie — checked shirtsleeves rolled up past his elbows and a wool tie neatly at the collar and tucked in at the third button. He was a man from another time.

Pauline was a woman of her time. She hadn't had the leisure for a relationship. She had been a career woman all her life. She noted there was no such thing as a career man. She had made her choices. No regrets. But there were losses. There always are.

* * *

'You get it, Tony, don't you? New starts for old.'

'But Xeno has his own son. He has a wife. What will she say?'

'She's not his wife. They have an arrangement. You want to give me a lecture on family values or will you take the cash and do the job?'

'When do I have to leave?'

'That's more like it! I'll fly you Business Class. Book a decent car at the airport. Get you a new suit. Looking the part is half the battle. Say you're her grandfather. Be confident.'

'But when do I leave?'

'Soon. Soon. And Tony, if you say anything — one word — to Pauline, no deal, OK?'

Tony felt uneasy. He trusted Pauline. He didn't trust Leo. So why . . . ? But he put the thought aside.

Getting a passport for Perdita was easy. Leo was on the birth certificate as her father. MiMi had registered the birth. Even the photograph was simple because Pauline kept emailing them to him.

Leo hadn't seen MiMi for three months. Milo spent half his time at Pauline's with his mother and the other half at home with Leo. Leo explained this as MiMi needing time to get better.

'Why can't she get better with us?'

'She will do . . . soon.'

'So Leo,' said Pauline, barging into his office as she always did, the cunt, 'how long is this going to go on?'

Leo didn't look up. 'Is that a real question?'

'Can you stop behaving like a shmendrick and get a DNA test so that we can all stop this?'

'I didn't start it. I can't stop it.'

'You need to know the truth.'

'I don't need to know what I know.'

'You some kind of psychic?'

'Can't you ever shut up?'

'Why don't you ask me how your wife is? Or do you know that via your spooky psychic powers too?'

Leo got up. At least he was much taller than Pauline.

'How's MiMi?'

'How do you think she is?'

'I have no idea — you told me to ask — so tell me.'

'She's fragile, hurt, humiliated. I'd never talk to you again if I were her.'

'She isn't talking to me.'

'She's still there for you, Leo, even after all the murdering. Why won't you take a DNA test?'

'So that MiMi can have her humiliation written on a piece of paper?'

'What, you want to hang it round her neck with a giant letter A for Adulterer written on it?'

'The baby is Xeno's.'

'I don't know how to handle this madness, Leo. Look, just come over later, will you? Sit down. Talk. Please . . . '

'Does MiMi want to talk to me?'

'Just come over.'

★ ★ ★

Leo left work early. He picked Milo up from school. 'Is Mummy coming home with us today?'

'Not today. I'm coming with you to see Mummy.'

Milo was pleased. They talked about football in the car and Leo promised to take him to a game at the weekend. By the time he got to Pauline's he had almost forgotten, or some part of him had forgotten, that MiMi had left him, or had he left her? He couldn't remember.

As he parked the Range Rover and Milo went running up the steps, Leo saw MiMi in the window. The short, dark, heavy hair. The red lipstick. She was wearing an oversized check shirt. He stood still, just looking at her. He realised his face was wet. Was it raining?

'Daddy! Come on!'

Leo followed Milo in. MiMi bent and kissed her son, ruffled his hair. 'Go and get changed and see you in the kitchen. Go on! *Dépêche-toi!*'

Milo hesitated — his father still at the door, his mother at the foot of the stairs.

Neither parent spoke. Milo stood between them like a lighthouse between the rocks and the shipwreck.

★ ★ ★

MiMi opened the door into the drawing room. Leo followed behind her. He lifted his hand, put it down. He lifted his hand and touched her shoulder. She flinched. *She doesn't want me.*

She took something from the console table, turned and gave it to Leo. It looked like a letter.

'I can't talk to you, Leo. Not yet. Pauline . . . she only wants the best for us. I said I'd see you and then I realised I can't. I wrote you this.'

Milo came running down the stairs in his tracksuit. He saw his parents. He felt it all. His open face closed. He went quietly down to the kitchen.

'He's confused,' said MiMi.

'I want him to live with me,' said Leo.

'Pardon?'

'I want custody of Milo.'

Even as Leo was saying what he said he couldn't believe that such idiot words could come out of the idiot mouth in his idiot face when all he wanted to do was put his arms round his wife and cry until his tears made a river that would float them both away from this landlocked place.

MiMi left the room.

Leo opened the letter.

Dear Leo,

Does time make fools of us all? I was not easy to marry, I know that. I tried not to marry you because neither of us have a happy-ever-after story written inside us. We both come from broken families. We are wary as wild animals.

116

You made your way the way men do in the outside world. I was lucky because I have music. Music is the world inside me. I am a performer, but whether or not I perform, the music is there.

I know you find me hard to read. We used to joke that you never learned to read music. You said right at the beginning of our relationship that men find women impossible to know. Do you remember?

Do I know you? I thought I did. I know the way you are vulnerable and fearless all at the same time. The way that nothing seems too hard for you. The way you grab life. Your big mouth.

I have felt safe with you and that was unexpected. I don't feel safe any more and that is making me ill.

Did you not want this baby? Why not? Why did we not talk about that? I thought when you saw her you would love her.

These last few months I was sure you were having an affair. You have been so distant. And all the time you thought I was having an affair. And all the time neither of us spoke. I guess I had decided to wait until you got over it. Or came in one day to tell me you were leaving.

I am married to you, Leo. I would not use Xeno to end our marriage. If I no longer loved you I would leave you. Do you not know that about me? Not even that?

And do you not know that about him?

Is it because you would do such things

that you imagine it is what I am doing to you? What he is doing to you?
When did I lose your love?

Leo put down the letter. There was an old note folded in the envelope. A wine stain on the back. He opened it. It was his handwriting.

1. Can I live without you? Yes.
2. Do I want to? No.
3. Do I think about you often? Yes.
4. Do I miss you? Yes.
5. Do I think about you when I am with another woman? Yes.
6. Do I think that you are different to other women? Yes.
7. Do I think that I am different to other men? No.
8. Is it about sex? Yes.
9. Is it only about sex? No.
10. Have I felt like this before? Yes and no.
11. Have I felt like this since you? No.
12. Why do I want to marry you? I hate the idea of you marrying someone else.
13. You are beautiful.

Leo stood in Pauline's wide-windowed drawing room. There was a piano in the bay. Pauline had played since she was a girl. On the music stand were some practice pieces of Milo's. Then he saw the manuscript paper. MiMi was writing a song. What were the words? '*Abandon ship, baby. Before it's too late. Jump ship, baby, don't wait. The threat's not yours, it's mine.*

118

We're caught in a gap of time.'

Scribbled on the top was 'PERDITA'.

Leo took it.

★   ★   ★

A week later Tony was gardening at Pauline's when she came out of the house carrying the baby. 'Is Leo home? He isn't answering his phone.'

'He's home,' said Tony. 'Keeps himself to himself these days, y'know.'

'There's an old saying,' said Pauline. 'What's past help should be past grief.'

'That's Shakespeare,' said Tony.

'*The Winter's Tale*,' said Pauline.

She went down to the Audi on the drive. Tony put down his fork and, coming after her, said — too suddenly, because he had been thinking about it for days — 'Would you like to go to a movie tonight?'

'Do you mean me?' said Pauline.

'Yes, I do,' said Tony.

'Because you were looking straight into that bush,' said Pauline.

Tony looked at the gravel. 'There's a Lauren Bacall season on at the Everyman. Tonight is *To Have and Have Not*.'

'I'd like that,' said Pauline. 'Yes.'

★   ★   ★

Tony watched Pauline drive away. He could feel his heart beating.

* ★ ★

Leo opened the front door. Pauline was holding the baby.

'I told you not to try any sentimental stunts,' said Leo.

Pauline handed Leo the sleeping baby. Leo held her away from him like she was on fire.

'I trusted them and they betrayed me.'

'You trusted them because they love you.'

'One big, happy family. In your dreams, Pauline.'

'Why are you obsessed with this madness?'

'Madness? You call it madness. You say they don't love each other? The way they touch, talk, whisper, dance? When he's here he's always with her. And I liked it.'

'So what if they are a little bit in love with each other?'

'You admit it, then?'

'Would you rather they disliked each other? Were indifferent to each other? Is it because you have slept with both of them?'

'Who told you that?'

'Xeno's quite open about it.'

'Well, I'm not. We were schoolboys.'

'Are you jealous of him or of her?'

'Spare me the TV psychoanalysis.'

'Leo, you are the father of this child. MiMi is faithful. Xeno is your friend. Take a DNA test. And put things right. There is still a chance to do right.'

Leo heard her. Chance to do right. Chance to do right. Chance to do right. The baby woke and

120

struggled in his arms. He passed her back to Pauline.

'Why is she called Perdita?'

'It means little lost one.'

'I'll come to the house tomorrow. We'll go and take a test. OK?'

Strangely to Some Place

That evening Pauline and Tony went to the Everyman Cinema.

Pauline was wearing a pretty dress and Tony had brushed his sports jacket. He bought the cinema tickets even though Pauline could have bought the cinema.

They sat upright and formal in the comfy couple seats. Pauline realised that she never went to the movies because it made her feel sorry for herself. She thought about her mother's parents, fleeing Nazi Germany and starting a salt-beef bar in the East End. It was a hard life but a happy marriage. Her mother trained as a nurse and married a dentist. Pauline had gone to an academic girls' school, then to university, then into investment banking. Refugees to riches in three generations. But she hadn't met anyone she liked well enough to be with. She knew her parents worried about her; about being lonely, old, uncared for.

Now, sitting next to Tony studiously watching Lauren Bacall and making sure his body was a clear three inches away from hers, she suddenly moved close to him. Very slowly he took her hand.

Afterwards, walking back down the hill from the cinema in Hampstead towards Pauline's house in Belsize Park, she asked Tony what he liked to do at weekends. 'Go walking,' he said. 'I feel better outside. I'm going to Kew Gardens tomorrow.'

Pauline did not really believe in walking; first there were legs, then there were bicycles and now there were cars. But she thought she might give it a try.

At her front door Tony thanked her for the evening. They agreed to meet the following day. They stood smiling at each other under the street lamp. Neither of them knew what to do next. She touched his arm, nodded and went up the path to the front door. He watched till she was safely inside.

Pauline looked at herself in the hall mirror. She thought she'd pop to the chemist in the morning and get a new lipstick.

★   ★   ★

When Tony got home, strangely, or not strangely, light-hearted, there was a message on his answer machine.

Tomorrow. Heathrow. Twelve noon.

★   ★   ★

The next morning Leo got up early. His mind felt clean and clear. For the first time in weeks, months, he could stop thinking because at last he knew what to do.

The emptiness of the house that had seemed hateful to him now seemed like a space to create something new. What had happened could unhappen.

126

Manor Park Library

ITEMS ISSUED/RENEWED
FOR Mazidur Chowdhury
ON 22/07/17 14:29:56
AT Manor Park Library (NEW)

Gap of time/Winterson, Jeanette
90800000136744 DUE 12/08/17
Like father, like son/Allen, Diane
90800000136908 DUE 12/08/17
2 item(s) issued

Free Public Wi-Fi is now available at this branch.
Please speak to a member of staff for more
information.
Thank you - Manor Park Library

Leo arrived an hour early at Pauline's. He was shaved, dressed; he seemed different, better.

Pauline was wondering if she needed walking boots to go to Kew Gardens. And what were those things people wore in the country? Barbours?

'Kew Gardens is a park,' said Leo.

'Well, all right,' said Pauline, 'but Jews don't do rain. It makes us nervous. Look what happened to Noah.'

'Who are you going with?' asked Leo.

'I've got a date. What's it to ya?'

'So you'll be out all day?'

Pauline nodded. 'MiMi's taken Milo swimming. She won't be back till eleven.'

'I know. He told me.'

'Leo — I'd like to pop up to the chemist before we go for the test. Will you look after Perdita for half an hour?'

'No problem, Pauline. Give her to me.'

He was charming Leo, smiling Leo, persuasive Leo. Pauline grabbed her handbag and went on her errand.

As soon as he was sure she was out of the way, Leo let himself out of the house and got back into his car. In his car was a wine box with a blanket in it. He laid the baby down. She started to cry. He put the radio on.

* * *

Tony was waiting at the entrance to Terminal 5. Leo gave him the passport and a bag. 'Nappies.

Formula milk. Clean clothes. Rash cream. All the shit. You know how to change a baby, don't you? If not someone on the plane will help you. I've texted you Xeno's address and phone number. You're booked on the return flight on Monday. Call me if there are any problems. Better go — plane leaves in an hour.'

★ ★ ★

And then everything happened in slow motion and too fast.

★ ★ ★

MiMi and Pauline driving to the house in Little Venice.

MiMi running from room to room, shouting LEO! LEO!

Milo on his own at Pauline's when the phone rang and it was Tony.

Milo heard the answer machine: 'Pauline, it's Tony. I can't go to Kew today. I'm on my way to the airport. Sorry.'

Milo called Pauline to tell her. He could hear his mother in the background. 'Why is Tony at the airport?'

Milo put down the phone. *There was a man lived in an airport.*

Soon after, the doorbell rang. It was Leo.

'Mummy's looking for you,' said Milo.

'We're going away for a few days. To Munich. See Granddad.'

'Is Mummy coming?'

'No.'

'I'll stay here, I think,' said Milo.

Leo was angry. 'We're going together. I've packed for you. Get whatever you want from here — not too much — and come on.'

In the car Milo was silent. Then he said, 'Where's Perdita?'

'She's fine.'

Leo had booked a flight to Berlin. He wasn't planning to see his father. He just wanted to get away. And when they got back, MiMi would have realised that everything was for the best.

But MiMi had already called the police to say that her husband was trying to leave the country with their baby.

'I don't see how Tony's involved,' said Pauline. 'His phone's going straight to voicemail.'

★ ★ ★

Leo was in the queue at Passport Control. The man checking documents asked him to stand aside a moment. The next thing he knew, three policemen were asking what he'd done with the baby.

Then it happened.

Leo arguing with the police. The police arguing with Leo. All big guys. All at the same height. The little Indian passport-checker was trying to pretend that nothing was happening as he processed other people coming through, all staring at Leo.

The police were confused because Leo had no baby. Leo said his wife had post-natal depression. He was taking their son on holiday to give

her a break. The police looked at Milo's passport
— is this your father? Yes.

The big guys went back to arguing — no one
cared about Milo.

There was a man lived in an airport.

Milo moved steadily, quietly backwards, away
from them, their backs to him in an angry circle.
No one would notice.

Milo was round the corner and going towards
the security lanes. There was a family over in
Lane Four. He ran over to them — if anyone saw
him they thought he was just catching up. He
put his backpack on the metal conveyor belt. He
walked through the metal detector. He looked
round. He was in the airport. Maybe he could
find Tony.

Kites Ravens Wolves Bears

Tony was in New Bohemia.

He liked the palm trees planted down the middle of the roads. He wondered if there was a botanical gardens. He had a free day tomorrow before his flight.

The sky was low and overcast. The heat was as close and intense as a sauna. He took off his suit jacket but he didn't loosen his tie. He didn't want to look sloppy.

Supermoon tonight, the man at the car rental told him. She's closer to the earth than normal — gonna be weather with her. Nice baby.

Tony got in the BMW. It was not like his Nissan. He thought he might use some of the £50,000 to buy a new car. Pauline had an Audi. She wouldn't want to be driven about in a Nissan. He had a feeling he should have told Pauline what he was doing.

Wide freeways. Tall buildings. Billboards advertising primetime TV shows. Square, miserable social housing hung over the fast, hostile roads. Flophouses on the outskirts of the city. Drive in for $40 a room, 2 sharing. All-u-can-eat breakfast. He idled in traffic on the bridge. The construction work covered his windscreen in cement dust like talcum powder. He could smell fried onions and diesel.

As he drove into the heart of the city he heard

music everywhere — from cars, buildings, street corners, bars. Two boys were washing car windscreens at the traffic lights. One was sitting on an upturned metal bucket drumming on the bucket in front of him with the Squeezee. Tony was nervous and exhilarated; he'd never been out of England. The only holidays he took were walking holidays in Scotland.

★ ★ ★

Tony pulled into the car park of the bank. They were expecting him. They took him into a private room, checked his passport and the documents from Leo and gave him the money in a case. He signed for it. He asked them if they could direct him to a particular address. One of the younger men on the team seemed watchful and shifty. He wrote down the address. Said he'd look it up. Tony didn't like him.

When Tony got back to the car, Perdita was whimpering in small, exhausted gulps. He had left her on the back seat because he didn't know what else to do. He had bundled his coat in the footwell in case she rolled over.

The baby had cried a lot on the plane. The British Airways staff had changed her for him and fed her but she was complaining deeper than food and sleep and wetness. Tony wondered if it was all right to take a baby from its mother so soon.

At least she would soon be with her father.

Tony sat in the back of the car and called the number Leo had given him for Xeno. It was disconnected. Tony called Leo. There was no answer.

Perdita was crying full-throttle now so Tony started to sing to her in Spanish. She seemed to like that. Tony added the velvet bag Leo had given him to the money in the case. And there was a piece of sheet music to go in too. He put it all together, sang a bit more until the baby fell asleep, then he drove to the address in his wallet.

It wasn't far out of town. A pretty suburb. The house was old colonial-style with an ironwork balcony over the first storey. There was an SUV on the drive. Tony got out. The rain had stopped. He could hear thunder somewhere but a long way off.

He rang the doorbell. Xeno must be expecting him by now.

For a long time no one answered. Tony walked round the back with Perdita, admiring the subtropical planting. Then a woman appeared at the back door. Spanish by the look of her. She didn't speak English well so Tony spoke to her in Spanish. No, Mr Xeno not here. Los Angeles. No back till ten days.

Tony got on the phone again to Leo. Still no answer. He went back to the car, sitting in the front with the door open. He had only enough milk for one more feed. Hospital. He should take the baby to a hospital, just to get her fed and changed and checked out. They would do that. Then he'd go to the hotel and wait till he could speak to Leo.

It was when he was leaving Xeno's house that he noticed the car across the street.

★ ★ ★

At the hotel they were helpful. Yes, the room was pre-paid. Yes, the hospital was just a couple of miles away.

Tony was suddenly exhausted. He went upstairs with Perdita. He took off her Babygro, vest, nappy. She was red and chafed between the legs. He thought he would bath her. If she were a plant he would be watering her. Bathing was a kind of watering, wasn't it?

He ran the bath, carefully checking the temperature. He swung her in gently, sleeves rolled up, kneeling on the floor. He held her in both hands in the water, swooshing her back and forth. His mother must have done this to him, mustn't she? Before the water dried up and there was no more love.

The baby seemed to like being bathed. Maybe I could have been a father, he thought. But that would have needed a mother . . .

Once she was dried and changed and fed, Tony lay down with her on the bed. They both fell deeply asleep.

★ ★ ★

It was the door to his room opening that woke him. The room was dark. He saw the light from the corridor. A man's shape. Someone from the hotel? The person was coming in but they didn't put on the light. 'Hello?' he called. 'Hello?' He reached out and flipped down the overhead switch. There was a man there in an anorak. The door closed swiftly as he left. What was the time?

Already midnight.

He checked his phone — nothing from Leo. No messages on the hotel phone either. He sent a text: CALL TONY. URGENT.

Perdita was stirring. He must get her food. He showered and shaved as though it were morning, even though it was late at night. He put his trousers in the trouser press. Clean shirt. He was about to leave with the sleepy, grumbling baby when he decided to take the attaché case.

Downstairs it was just the night staff on the desk. He asked for his car to be brought round. Outside, waiting for his car, the baby in his arms, he saw the moon. He had never seen the moon so big. She looked like she was coming in to land. The moon lit up the baby in his arms like a pearl.

★　★　★

He set off towards the Sainta Maria hospital.

As he drove away from the hotel he saw that car again. He knew it was the same one.

At the first red light he tried to see them in the mirror. Two men.

He tried a few turns — the car stayed with him; yes, this was trouble.

At the hospital he pulled into the disabled parking right at the door, took Perdita and the case and went in. The bright lights disoriented him but there was a friendly man on the desk and when he explained, and said he would pay, there appeared to be no problem with his strange midnight request.

A nurse soon came down, swinging up Perdita with expert femaleness. The nurse seemed to believe all his story about being the grandfather, bringing the baby back to his son, son's flight late, mother unwell. Yes, unwell.

'We have a BabyHatch here,' said the nurse, 'saddest thing you ever saw but better than being left on a street corner or in a tram car, I guess.'

'A child should be wanted,' said Tony.

'Yes, sir,' said the nurse, her quick fingers changing and dressing Perdita. The nurse gave Tony a couple of bottles of formula milk to heat up and a spare set of nappies. It would be enough till they got the plane home, he thought. They could go to the botanic gardens after all.

He was heading down the steps towards his car when he saw them. Two of them. In the shadows near the BMW. They hadn't seen him yet — they were leaning against a truck, smoking. He knew they were waiting for him.

He went back in. There was an exit sign pointing to the side of the hospital. He'd go that way. Leave the car. Get a cab.

As he came out of the hospital the sky split and the rain started. The baby was crying. He took off his suit jacket and wrapped her up. This was crazy. The water was so thick it was splashing up to his knees. He should go back in. He ran back to the exit door but it was a one-way only. He rattled the wet bar, already soaked through. He kept on walking round the building — he couldn't risk the front entrance. Then he saw it lit up.

The BabyHatch.

It was a five-second lifetime decision. He opened the hatch. He could feel the gentle warmth. He unwrapped Perdita from his jacket and put her in. Then he put the attaché case in with her. He could hardly see what he was doing with the rain making him into a waterfall, but he closed the hatch just enough so that he could open it again, wedging his pen in the top where it would have closed shut. All he had to do now was get to the car and come back for her. They were after the money. He'd tell them it was in the hotel. Give them his key. Then he'd drive straight to the airport. He had his passport in his jacket. The rest didn't matter.

★ ★ ★

The hospital car park was quiet. Tony reached his car. There was no one around. He turned onto the street and that was when the headlights hit him from the front. He reversed. The car came after him. He swerved direct again, put his foot down to pull away and heard the shot. Then the wheel jerked out of his hands as the front tyre burst and he hit the wall.

The men were at the car.

One of them dragged him out. Hit him. Hit him again. The other one was searching the car. Tony hit back, lost his footing in the water that was over his shoes; he fell, knocked his head. As he was losing consciousness he heard another

car. Another shot. Someone took his hand.
'Pauline,' he said or thought he said.
　'We should wait for the cops.'
　'He's dead.'

Interval

So many stories of lost and found.

As though the whole of history is a vast Lost Property Department.

Perhaps it began when the moon splintered off from the earth, pale, lonely, watchful, present, unsocial, inspired. Earth's autistic twin.

And all the stories of twins begin. Pairs who can't be separated but can't be together. Of shut-outs and lock-outs, and feuds and broken hearts and lovers who think they are immortal until one of them dies.

Paradise stories — part moon, part womb. Two planets spinning off in space. The mother-ship. Atlantis. Eden. Heaven. Valhalla. Brave new world. There must be another world.

We set off in boats. The stars were lights on the tops of the masts. We didn't know that stars are like fossils, imprints of the past, sending light like a message, like a dying wish.

We set off in boats, thought we'd sail to the rim of the world and slip over the edge like a raft on a waterfall, spinning to the place we knew existed, if we dared to find it.

It must be here somewhere.

The missingness of the missing. We know what that feels like. Every endeavour, every kiss, every stab in the heart, every letter home, every leaving, is a ransack of what's in front of us in the service of what's lost.

In the sky, Planet Moon is 239,000 miles away.

That's not far when you remember that the sun is 93 million miles away.

But if you were standing on red Mars it would look as though blue earth and pale moon were twins sitting side by side, heads together, bent over a book. Never separated in time.

The moon controls earth's tides. The daily ebb and flow of our life here. And because of the moon, earth's climate is stable. Moon's gravitational pull means that earth doesn't wobble too much. Scientists call it obliquity. The moon holds us fast.

★ ★ ★

The early separation of earth-moon, hundreds of millions of years before life of any kind happened on earth, has no reason to be the grand motif of our imagination. But it is.

There are thirteen moons every calendar
year.
They measure time differently on the
moon.
The moon orbits the earth once every 28
days
As though she's looking for something she
lost.
A long time ago.

Two

Traffic

Saturday morning. Spring day.

★ ★ ★

The Fleece occupied a high plot of ground with a long view down to a small road that led, winding and particular, to the highway. Beyond lay the river, like possibilities, like plans, wide as life when you are young and don't know that plans, rivers, possibilities must sooner or later empty into the ocean beyond.

But today there is no beyond.

The long tables in the garden were spread with white cloths. Over the tables were light steel frames hung with Chinese lanterns to be lit when the sun went down.

Clo had repainted the peeling benches, burnt and sweated in the heat, and spliced new ropes on the swingboats where the couples liked to sway, lazy in the lowering sun.

★ ★ ★

Perdita had kicked Clo out of his bed early that morning and sent him shopping.

'What am I supposed to buy him?'

'Use your imagination!'

'That's real cruel because I don't do imagination!'

149

Clo was over six feet tall and built like a wrestler. Baseball cap on backwards, shades slotted down the front of his T-shirt, jeans stuffed into oversized skater boots, he was throwing cushions around searching for his phone when Perdita handed it to him. 'I put the list of stuff in your phone,' she said. 'Buy what we need, and then — just see what happens.'

'You'd better pray for me that something happens.'

Perdita poured him coffee. Clo drank it down. 'How come you run this household?'

'You want the job?'

Clo looked down onto the top of her head — he was at least a foot taller than Perdita. He gave her a hug. She hugged him back. He was turning to go. 'Hey — what you get Dad for his birthday?'

'A harmonica,' said Perdita.

'Why didn't I think of that?'

★　★　★

Clo got into his Chevy Silverado, dropped his shades, turned up the music, slid down the window and set off along the winding dust road to the highway. The skyline of the city broke the horizon line in the distance. The early sun reflecting off the steel and glass turned the buildings into gold ingots. The air was fresh and starting to warm.

Saturday morning. Spring day.

EXIT HERE FOR AUTOS LIKE US:

It was the first turn off the highway as you left Bear County.

There was a sign:

PICK A CAR! ANY CAR!

Autolycus was a dealer. A wheeler-dealer. A dealer in wheels. A soapbox salesman with a silver tongue.

Autolycus. Part Budapest, part New Jersey. Chutzpah of Old Europe meets chutzpahdick of the New World.

Autolycus: ponytail, goatee beard, cowboy boots, string tie. Part crook, part sage.

★   ★   ★

It was the up-wing doors of the DeLorean that Clo saw as he drove along the highway in his Chevy. Clo pulled in ahead of the DeLorean and got out. Autolycus was bending over the rear engine. Steam from the radiator and gasket head hid what was left of his tiny body not concealed by the up-shot gull-wing doors of the car.

'Is that the car from that movie *Back to the Future?*'

Autolycus straightened up, his eyes reading Clo's amiable, open face as he stood, sunglasses in hand, tall over the low-slung car and its high-strung owner.

'You got a hammer?'

'You want to use a hammer on a car like this?'

'I want to use it to smash my head in. I was

screwed by the guy who sold it to me. I'm too honest.'

'I can give you a ride if you want.'

'That's a pretty truck you got there. I like a Chevy. Brand-new.'

'Yeah — we had a good year last year at the Fleece. You been there?'

'The Fleece? That's your place?'

'Sure is — so, it's my Dad's place, but I'm his son.'

Autolycus swabbed his hands on a medicated rag, locked up the DeLorean and hopped into the Chevy. 'Stitched leather — and so clean. I like this.'

'Dad always said, no matter how old or beaten-up your car, you keep it smart. I learned that lesson when we was poor and now we're rich.'

'And I thought the American dream was done, and only the rich got richer — or politicians.'

'Don't get me wrong — we're just a family business, but yeah, it's a good business.'

'So where you heading, big guy?'

'Down town. It's Dad's seventieth birthday today. We're having a party. My little sister sent me out to get a few things and maybe a special gift for him, like a son would get his dad. I said, what the Holy Lion of Judah am I supposed to get him?'

'You religious? He religious?'

'I was raised on the Good Book. We don't do church so much these days but I still believe that God has his ways.'

'You believe that God sends us what we need?'

'Sure do — Dad always says my little sister was sent by God, even if she's a pain in the ass.'

Autolycus nodded. 'I guess this is one of those God-sent days too. God sent me to you.'

'I'm the one that's helping you out!'

Autolycus nodded again — he cocked his head sideways and took a flask from one of his pockets. He swigged. 'You want bourbon?'

'I want to keep my licence.'

'My doctor says I have to drink every day for my liver.'

'Go right ahead.'

'So what's your name?'

'Clo.'

'Good to meet you, Clo. A good day and that's a fact.'

★ ★ ★

Saturday morning. Spring day.

★ ★ ★

Perdita saw her father on a ladder, hammer in his hand, nails in his mouth. She had thought he was still sleeping. She put on fresh coffee and went into the garden to wish him happy birthday.

Over the years Shep had worked hard to build up the bar. The Fleece served food; the best fish soups, crabs in their shells, rice and peas, black beans. If it was a way out to drive, along the levee where the cormorants prophesied the weather, well, the drive was worth it.

In the beginning Shep had done most of the work himself; restoring the long shutters, finding lengths of iron balustrade to rebuild the balcony that ran all the way round the building.

He had worked with Perdita strapped to his back. She had been put down once and he was never going to let her be put down again. At night she slept in his room and he told her old stories of love and loss. She was too young to know that's what they were. What she knew was the sound of his voice.

As she grew, Shep taught Perdita piano and harmony and they listened to the music Shep had grown up on himself — girl groups like the Marvelettes, protest songs, Dylan and Baez, and Shep's favourite, Marvin Gaye.

★　★　★

Perdita went out into the garden. Her father was watching the buzzards wing-level with the wind.

'Happy birthday, Dad.'

He put his arm round her. 'I have something for you.'

'For me? It's your birthday — not mine.'

Out of his pocket Shep pulled a soft, worn leather pouch.

'This came from your mother. I was waiting till you turned eighteen, but instead I turned seventy. Didn't want to drop dead and not give this to you myself.'

'You're not dropping dead.'

'Here.' Shep emptied the contents of the pouch in her hands.

Perdita sat silently, looking at the shining cold-fire beauty — the making of the world. A layer of time. That's what diamonds are.

'Are they real?'

'Sure. Diamonds all the way.'

'She wasn't poor, then.'

'I don't reckon she was a poor woman, no.'

Perdita was holding the diamonds that her mother had held as her mother must once have held her, in both hands.

She started to cry.

'Don't cry,' said Shep. 'You were loved then and you are loved now. Isn't that enough?'

Perdita nodded and wiped her eyes with the back of her hand. She was at that age when sometimes she was a grown woman and sometimes she was still a kid.

'I'll put it on this afternoon,' she said, 'for your party.'

'I don't know why we're having a party. It's a lot of fuss.'

'What's the point of being old if you can't party?'

'Am I old?'

'Yeah, you're old.' She kissed him. 'But you're not dying.'

'Maybe I'm old, but I'm still a better dancer than you.'

She reached up and swatted him — Shep was tall like Clo, and a foot taller than Perdita. Then she took his hand and they sang and danced together for a minute — Shep on melody and clicking his fingers, Perdita singing over the top in harmony. *Fly me to the moon, let me play among the stars . . .*

'Was my mother a good dancer?'

'She was a good singer. She wrote you that song. The first one I ever taught you.'

'Did she really write it?'

'That's her music notation in her handwriting. That's her piano part. She was a cool musician. That song was her letter to you. You want to sing it later?'

Perdita stopped dancing and shook her head. 'I'll sing all your favourites.'

'Let's go inside and run through a few on the piano. Are the girls here yet?'

'Not yet, Dad. It's early.'

Shep nodded. 'I guess it is. I didn't sleep last night. Mortality was visiting me.'

'You're fine!'

'High blood pressure.'

'So why not leave the work to me and Clo?'

'Surest way to die is to stop working.'

'What did she die of? My mother?'

Shep put his arms round Perdita. 'You know I don't know.'

'You kept these diamonds all these years and you never told me. Maybe there's other things you never told me.'

Shep laughed. 'Sweetheart, if I knew the who and the where and the why and how — why wouldn't I tell you?'

'Would you?'

Perdita didn't know anything about the BabyHatch. All she knew was that her mother had died and that Shep had adopted her. From a church a long way away. The past was a long way

156

away. Nearly eighteen years' drive.

Whenever she asked about her mother Shep said, 'She was a damn fine woman.'

When she asked about her father, he said, 'I don't know about him at all.'

When she asked her brother, Clo, he said, 'Ask Dad.'

So she had stopped asking questions because there weren't any answers.

Overhead the buzzards circled round their cold, high cry, circling as if they were looking for something they had lost. A long time ago.

⋆　⋆　⋆

Saturday morning. Spring day.

⋆　⋆　⋆

Out on the highway Clo had the radio up full-blast like he was trying to blow up the car from the inside with a double-barrelled bass. As they pulled up towards the stop lights, the Chevy booming, its metal flanks pulsing, Autolycus put his hands to his mouth and yelled —

'OK, big guy! Exit here towards the roundabout!'

Clo pulled into the exit lane. 'I hate roundabouts! They were just coming in when I was a kid. I like a road straight ahead of me. Stop sign now and again to take a drink. Cruise control. No stress, no steering.'

Clo didn't look like a man who did much steering, leaning his forearms on the wheel, his big hands drumming to the beat.

Autolycus took another swig from his flask and put on his shades against the reflecting sun.

'Let me tell you something for nothing that no highwayman ever will tell you, ever will know. You listenin'?'

Clo turned the sound down and the car stopped reverberating.

'Here's the truth . . . if roundabouts had been invented sooner the whole of western civilisation would be different.'

'The whole thing?'

'Whole damn thing.'

'How'd y'work that out?'

'Remember the story of Oedipus?'

'Eddy who?'

'Guy who murdered his father and married his mother.'

'Was that on 'Fox News'?'

'It happened a while back. Oedipus is racing up some narrow road when he meets an old guy in a chariot.'

'A Chevy Chariot?'

'No, just a chariot. So the old guy, Laius, is a King and he won't give way to some kid, and Oedipus is a moody type, proto-democrat, not impressed with age or chariots, and he won't give way either. The two of 'em fight — and Eddy ends up killing the old guy.'

'Did he have a concealed-weapons licence?'

'He just hit him over the head.'

'That's not respectful.'

'Just listen! The whole mess happened at a crossroads, right? Three roads running into one.

If we had invented the roundabout in time, the calamity could never've happened. First it's you, then it's me, y'know?'

'Yeah, OK, so what?'

'So what? Freud so what? Biggest theory in psychoanalysis and the western world and you say so what?'

'Well, I never heard of it.'

'Oedipus complex! Men are always killing their fathers and marrying their mothers.'

'No, that ain't so! I don't know not a soul who's done that even once.'

'You can't do it more'n once. How many sets of parents you got?'

'I mean I never even heard of it — yeah, somebody sleeps with their sister maybe . . . yeah, that can happen, but . . . '

'Listen! It's a metaphor — rivalry and forbidden desire and the failure to leave behind the family romance.'

'You didn't say the King guy was his dad, and where was the mom — right up there in the Chevy?'

'It wasn't a Chevy! The mom was at home being Queen. Oedipus didn't know the old guy was his father. He was adopted. He had this curse on him that he would kill his parents, and as he liked his parents — they played with him when he was little and bought him a dog, y'know?'

'Sure, sure — my dad's like that.'

'So Eddy ran away from home. He didn't know he was adopted.'

'They never told him? My sister's adopted.

You gotta tell kids the truth.'

'That's right! So poor Eddy ran away to escape the curse and walked right into it — killing his own father.'

'That is some shit.'

'Yeah — so after he had murdered Laius he carried on to the city, fancy place called Thebes — bars, clubs, no two-bit shit — and he found that Thebes was being terrorISed, TErrorised, terrORised — like having the Mafia come to stay — by this creature called the Sphinx.'

'Sphinx? Isn't that underwear?'

'Spanx is underwear. The Sphinx was a woman — you know the type: part monster, part Marilyn Monroe. The Sphinx had her own kind of female logic — made plenty of sense to her but sounds pretty crazy to the rest of us. This was her deal: sit down, have a drink, do a quiz, and if you get the right answer she'll hand over control of Thebes — she had other business interests elsewhere. But because she was a tricky badass, if you got her question wrong she bit your head off.'

'I know that type! Do I know that type!'

'But Oedipus got the question right and part of his reward was to marry the Queen — which he could do as her husband was now dead. But the Queen was his own mother!'

'I feel sorry for the guy. Then what happened?'

'Oedipus and Jocasta, the mom, had four kids together, two boys and two girls. Nice family. Some mental instability but that's incest for you. On the whole they were OK. Then a plague plagued the city and some meddling oracle announced that the plague would never, ever end unless the killer of the dead old King was found. They had no idea about viruses in those days. Plagues were sent from the gods.'

'They said that about AIDS. Even I knew it was a stupid thing to say and I'm no doctor.'

'One thing you notice about progress, kid, is that it doesn't happen to everyone.'

'You are right there, brother — look at that piece of junk driving in front of us.'

'Probably made in Thebes, boy. So Oedipus starts the hunt for the killer and the hunt led to . . . himself! Imagine how he felt.'

'Like shit.'

'Like shit. His wife, or his mother, or his wife/mother, Jocasta, she went into the bedroom — the bedroom! A lot of resonance there. She hangs herself. Oedipus cuts her down, unpins her brooch and stabs out his own eyes.'

'For real?'

'For real. And this entire event — crucial to western thought, a billion neurotics, a million shrinks and motherfuckers, literary theory, all that anxiety of influence . . . '

'You can get a jab for that now.'

'Influence is not the same as influenza.'

'I said I wasn't medical.'

'And specialist porn.'

'You mean MILF?'

'Spell it out, boy — Mothers I'd Like to Fuck.'

'Uh-huh . . . ' (and they both laughed) 'UH-HUH!'

'This entire event could not have happened if the world had invented the roundabout.'

'That is some shit.'

'But there's nothing deep or poetic about a roundabout, is there? I mean, nobody ever looks solemn and says, *I've reached a roundabout in my life*. No, it's crossroads all the way.'

'What are you talking about?'

'Next exit, kid, next exit. This is home.'

★ ★ ★

And Clo saw the sign 'AUTOS LIKE US'.

'Hey! Holy Ghost! I heard about you! You're Autolycus! You're famous! You got the Motormobile Museum. We were moving out of the city soon after you showed up — from Detroit, right?'

'Right! You want to see the museum?'

'I don't have time.'

'What's the point of time if you don't have any?'

★ ★ ★

Clo parked the Silverado. A slip of a boy, prettier than he was handsome, came back-firing out of the garage in an open-topped Jeep.

'She's running too high!' yelled Autolycus.

'That's because the engine is shit!' shouted the boy. He was wearing oil-stained overalls. A pair of heavy goggles hung round his neck. He killed the engine and got out.

'I need you to take the tow-truck for the DeLorean.'

'Again?'

162

'Clo ... this is Zel. My assistant,' said Autolycus. 'Kids these days are either built like bulldozers with brains like Tarmac or they got a college degree and want to polish fenders. He's one of those. Reads all the time.'

'My sister reads all the time too,' said Clo. 'Hey, haven't I seen you out at the Fleece?'

Zel was looking down at the floor as though it had something to tell him.

'Well, I like reading in a youth,' said Autolycus, 'makes the stories easier to tell. This Jeep here belonged to Ernest Hemingway.'

'The fuel can strapped on the side did,' said Zel.

Autolycus ignored him. 'A 1940 khaki beauty. Ernest Hemingway. Writer. Hemingway served as a major in the American Army, Second World War. He was in the Liberation of Paris. Drove right down the rue de l'Odéon looking for that bookstore, Shakespeare and Company.'

'I've heard of Shakespeare but I never knew he ran a bookstore.'

'I guess you don't read much, huh? Here — a keepsake.'

Autolycus pulled a battered paperback out of his hunter's jacket that seemed to be a series of pockets held together by his own body. '*The Sun Also Rises* by Ernest Hemingway.'

'Thanks. I'll give it to my little sister.'

'No. I have the gift of second sight — one day you'll thank me for this book. Now go ahead, take a look around — that's Marilyn Monroe's Pontiac over there; put your nose down real close and you can still smell Chanel N°5.'

As Clo ambled away, Autolycus grabbed Zel by his greasy overalls.

'You want to ruin me? He's buying the DeLorean.'

'Him?'

'I can sell anything to anybody — so long as they got the money. We need to ditch the DeLorean.'

'You are a crook.'

'I always wanted to be a crook. It's my vocation.'

'I can't pick up the DeLorean. I have to leave early today — I told you.'

'Because your dad's coming in? To pick up the Mercury?'

'It's a kit car with phony paperwork.'

'When you can tell me what's real, in a world of avatars and clones, mass production, reproduction, and 3D printing, then tell me what's a fake, smartass.'

'I don't care anyway. He deserves to waste his money. That's not why I'm leaving early.'

Zel was twenty-something, not much of the something. Slight frame, strong shoulders, mass of hair on his head tied back like a girl's. Hands he turned over to the palms when he was upset, frowning as if he could read the lines there and find a way out. He had been living at the garage for over a year. Turned up one day riding a British Royal Enfield saddle-seat motorcycle he had rebuilt himself.

Autolycus, who was no saint, had given the kid a job, and later, when he found him sleeping on the discarded foam of the repair cars, he'd given him a home of a kind too. Zel worked hard, read books, didn't go out much.

'You should make it up with him. He asks about you.'

'He's the parent. He can make it up with me.'

'I got five kids. I never see 'em.'

'You never told me you had kids.'

'What, we're in a relationship all of a sudden? I have to tell you about my kids? I'll tell you something else, more important: regrets come soon enough in life. Don't go hunting for them.'

'Enough about my dad, OK? You said I could use the MGB Roadster today.'

'I did? What for?'

Zel blushed. 'I have a date.'

'Who is she?'

'No one you will ever know.'

'Haven't I been a friend to you and this is how you treat me?'

Zel was silent. Then he said, 'I'm sorry. I . . . I think I'm nervous.'

Autolycus grinned and punched his shoulder. 'Nothing to be nervous about! She'll love ya. But there's no rear seats in the roadster. How ya gonna make out?'

Zel dropped his head. 'She's not that kind of girl.'

'Let's have no lying. That's only fit for politicians.'

'I need something easy on the gas. She's an environmentalist.'

'Then take her for a walk.'

'I worked all night to get it ready.'

Clo came out of the museum.

'All these cars here for rental?'

'Yes sir-ee. And the music comes with them. Zel! Turn on the radio in that whitewall, two-tone, flared-fin on its way to Thunder Alley!'

Zel leaned in and turned the Bakelite knob. 'Rock Around the Clock' blasted onto the forecourt. Autolycus spun Zel under his arm before the boy could back off.

'Clo, Clo — take your pick. Every rental costs just one dollar.'

'One dollar?'

'The other 500 or 1000 or 2000 bucks, whatever we charge, we write down as a donation to the Motormobile Museum. Cash is good if you got it. I like to stay on the wrong side of the law.'

Clo held out his hand. 'You know, it's been great meeting you an' all — I'll bring my dad — but I gotta go; I just had my little sister texting me, and . . . '

Autolycus stretched up and slapped both their foreheads like they were a pair of faulty light bulbs.

'I got an idea! For the gift! For your father!'

'What?'

'I'll sell you the DeLorean.'

'You said you was screwed!'

'I did, I did, I was, I was! I'll sell it to you half-price. I paid $100K. I shudda paid fifty. You can have it for twenty-five.'

'It's broken down on the highway!'

'I'll have it running in time for your party. Your dad is seventy, right?'

'Yeah, that's right.'

'Wouldn't he like to wind back the clock? Your little sister said use your imagination. Bet she wasn't thinking of a DeLorean. No sir-ee! That'll show her who of the two of you is boss. That car is more than a car — it's a Time Machine. You're buying Time and who wouldn't want the gift of time for their seventieth birthday?'

'You reckon?'

'I know it, I know it, I know it! Bingo! High five! Let's dance . . . '

Autolycus grabbed Clo by the hand and started jiving to 'Rock Around the Clock'. It was like dancing with a lighter flame in the wind.

'Hey! I don't dance with guys! You gay or something?'

'Do I look gay?'

'You gotta lotta hand movements.'

'I was trained in puppet theatre. CON-GRATULATIONS CLO!'

The Day of Celebration

'One! Two! Three! Four!'

★ ★ ★

'If you wanna know if he loves you so, it's in his kiss, that's where it is.'

The Separations were great. They had a sound they called Hillybilly Soul Banjo and snare-drum, girl-group harmonies, steel guitar played hard on pedal and plec. Tall bass, thumb- and finger-plucked, and a Pentecostal piano; every chord a call to Judgement Day. That was Shep.

They called themselves The Separations because Holly, Polly and Molly were BabyHatch kids. The group had started out as the Orphans but that was too sad.

Anyway, Perdita was literal-minded and HollyPollyMolly couldn't be orphans because orphans are children whose parents are dead. The girls were foundlings — but who wants a girl group called the Foundlings?

Then Holly read something at school about six degrees of separation and, as they were all fans of vinyl retro soul, like The Three Degrees . . . and as they had been separated from their parents, it was obvious.

The three girls, HollyMollyPolly, were Chinese triplets. No one ever found out who had left them in the BabyHatch in Guangzhou. They'd been adopted by English missionaries. Their father was a minister from High Wycombe who had ended up in a Baptist church in New Bohemia via a mission to China. He had his own ideas about the End of the World, and Shep didn't agree with them, but — Apocalypse or Armageddon — the two of them were friends.

HollyPollyMolly were a year older than Perdita. All the children had played together from the beginning, and in the beginning Shep took Perdita to church with him.

Holly had a stammer. It was Shep who noticed that when she sang she didn't stammer — and to help her feel less awkward he had started all the little girls singing those old soul songs while he played the piano.

He had more faith in those days — these last ten years he had lost faith in his faith. The world was getting darker, not brighter. The poor were poorer, the rich were richer. People were killing each other in the name of God. What kind of a God wanted his followers to act like they were gun-slung avatars jihading it through 'World of Warcraft'?

If this was the end of time then fire it right back into eternity and get it over with.

He supposed that the point of time was that it would end — if it went on forever then it wouldn't be time, would it?

What to believe? What to believe in?

But Perdita was a kind of faith in her own right. He believed in her.

★ ★ ★

172

HollyPollyMolly were zipping each other into their sleeveless V-neck girl-group stage-wear. Perdita was brushing her pink suede shoes with a toothbrush.

'So do you think I should date your brother?' said Holly. 'He's asked me out.'

'Clo? He's twice your age!'

'I like older men.'

'I don't think you should date a guy who's still living at home in his thirties,' said Polly.

'He's not living at home — he's managing a business.'

'He said that?' Perdita pulled a face in the mirror at Holly, who was fixing her lipstick.

'Well, I think he's cute.'

'He's not cute.'

'He's your brother. How would you know?'

'He votes Republican and he can't pass his accountancy exams.'

'I can add up for both of us. You're just being mean.'

'She's nervous. Her boyfriend's coming.'

'He's NOT my boyfriend!'

The girls put their heads together in a row and sang, '*And if you wanna know if she loves him so — it's in her kiss.*'

Perdita blushed and bent over to examine her shoes.

'Don't tease him, OK? He's shy.'

'Is it him who's shy or you?'

Perdita sat up. 'It's crazy. He's just a boy. I'm just a girl. It's so normal it's weird. It's like eating a boiled egg — do you ever eat a boiled egg and look down at your plate and think, eggcup, egg, spoon, toast, salt, and somewhere in the background, out of sight, some kind of a hen who laid this thing, and you think, this is weird?'

HollyPollyMolly were staring at her. Perdita guessed the egg thing had never happened to them.

She tried again. 'I'm not explaining it right — it's just that — wherever you look — all the movies, books, TV shows, songs. You know? You know how it goes. Boy meets Girl — *Romeo and Juliet*. Girl meets Boy — *The Great Gatsby*. Girl meets Gorilla — *King Kong*. Girl meets Wolf — *Little Red Riding Hood*. Girl meets Paedophile — *Lolita* — not so good. Boy meets Mother — *Oedipus Rex* — not so good. Boy meets Girl with problems — *Sleeping Beauty*, *Rapunzel*. Girl meets Boy with body issues — *The Frog Prince*.'

She stopped. HollyMollyPolly were still staring at her. Egg or no egg, she wasn't making sense.

'Let's stick with the singing,' she said.

⋆　⋆　⋆

Zel backed the tartan-red MGB Roadster out of the lot. He loved the wire wheels and chrome centre spinners and the big wooden steering wheel. The seats were deep scuffed leather.

It was a nice feature of the classic cars that the radios had a retro button. Pre-selected songs from any decade you wanted: 50s, 60s, 70s, 80s. Press it and what you heard from the square honeycomb grille in the dashboard was the past. '*I'm not in love so don't forget it . . .*'

★   ★   ★

Zel drove; wide roads, narrow roads, dirt roads, back roads, out-of-town roads. Roads that he imagined. Roads he hoped were real. He'd ridden this way before, leaving his motorcycle outside the bar and standing just inside the door. She sang on Fridays at the bar.

Everyone crowded in. He didn't. He could only look at her through the kaleidoscope cut-outs of the crowd.

Last week she had asked him to dance with her and he had shaken his head right down through his body like a dog caught in the rain.

She didn't know where he lived. She didn't have his phone or his Facebook. Sometimes he didn't come to the bar for a few weeks. Then he'd be there, standing at the back again, so clean, so upright, so still, like he was made of polished metal.

And he never knew what to say. She wanted to kiss the hesitation of his throat.

But she had asked him to the party and he had said 'Yes'.

And now he was standing at the gate, slicked-back and sweet-smelling, in clean Levi's and a white shirt so obsessively unwrinkled it looked like it had been ironed with Botox.

Perdita heard his car. Perdita saw him across the fence.

She moved back. Her heart was over-beating.

Why do I feel this way? And what is this way that I am feeling? How can something so personal and so private, like a secret between myself and my soul, be the same personal, private secret of the soul for everyone?

There's nothing new or strange or wonderful about how I feel.

I feel new and strange and wonderful.

⋆ ⋆ ⋆

And now they were standing either side of the welcome sign, looking at each other.

And she wished that everything that had to happen had happened. That time would intervene and free them. That they could begin.

And he wished he could touch her and everything would pass through him and she would know him and they would begin.

She said, 'Hi.'

He said, 'I brought you these flowers.'

⋆ ⋆ ⋆

Clo had finished the bunting and the flags. He was sitting with his sleeves rolled up, having a Diet Coke with HollyMollyPolly. They were so pretty. And only half his age. What was that old saying? Why have one at thirty-six when you can have two at eighteen? And here were three of them. I'm loving it.

⋆ ⋆ ⋆

Perdita and Zel came over with a plate of crabs and sardines.

'Hey! It's you, I knew it was you!' said Clo.

'You know him?' said Perdita to Zel.

Zel was wishing this wasn't happening but it was. 'He knows my boss.'

Holly had her iPad out. 'Can you shut up with the work talk? I found this quiz. Invented by some old, maybe dead white psychologist called Arthur Aron. It's called The Experimental Generation of Interpersonal Closeness.'

'Huh?'

'It means how to fall in love without really trying. You ask each other a set of questions and then you get married.'

'We're sisters — we can't get married.'

'ROFL.'

'And who are we supposed to be falling in love with anyway?'

'You can fall in love with me,' said Clo. 'I can take it.'

'Yeah, but can we?'

Polly in pink. Molly in jade. Leaning forward, bright and beautiful. All things. Holly in purple, the leader, her thick black hair down to her waist. She bongo'd the table.

'Come on, people! Thirty-six questions. Let's just start — if anybody feels like they are falling in lurve with Clo, put up your hand and we can stop. Perdita — are you in?'

Zel looked sideways at Perdita. She didn't look at him at all.

'All right, question one — 'Who would be your favourite dinner guest of all time any time?' '

POLLY: Martin Luther King.

MOLLY: Janis Joplin.

HOLLY: God.

MOLLY: You can't have GOD!

HOLLY: Why can't I have God?

POLLY: He doesn't eat, so what's the point of inviting him to dinner?

HOLLY: Where in the Bible does it say God doesn't eat?

MOLLY: Why would he want to eat? He's God.

HOLLY: Why would he not want to eat? If I were God I'd eat all the time 'cause you'd never put on weight.

POLLY: Can we SHUT UP about God?

HOLLY: OK, OK! Perdita, who's your guest?

PERDITA: Miranda.

MOLLY: Miranda who?

PERDITA: She's fictional. She lives in Shakespeare.

HOLLY: You can't have a fictional character.

PERDITA: Why not? Celebrities are fictional characters. Just because they are alive doesn't make them real.

CLO: That's too deep for me.

PERDITA: Anyway, she chose GOD, for God's sake.

CLO: Don't let Dad hear you takin' the name in vain.

PERDITA: Dad doesn't believe in God any more. Didn't he tell you?

CLO: WHAT?!?!?

HOLLY: We are playing a GAME! Let's try another question. 'When did you last sing?' That's easy. 'When did you last cry?' Uh-oh

178

. . . 'Why did you last cry?' That's too personal.

CLO: Sure it's personal! How can you fall in love if it's not personal?

HOLLY: Don't you know? I can't believe you don't know this! Nobody FALLS in love — love is a hot mix of sex and despair, sex because you gotta have it, despair because you're lonely. WHO you fall in love with is really irrelevant.

CLO: You can have sex with anybody . . .

HOLLY: Listen to him!

CLO: But love is different — Dad loved Mom like the moon loves the earth.

PERDITA: He always says so.

HOLLY: I'm just telling you the latest findings about love.

ZEL: But they don't know, do they? Who really knows anything about love?

Clo grabbed the iPad. ''Complete this sentence — I wish I had someone I could share a . . . ''

HOLLY: Dog with. Though it should be WITH WHOM I could share a dog. I wish I had a dog: a Labradoodle?

CLO: A dog? What about a joint? Cool date, low lights . . .

MOLLY: We already share all our clothes, so I'd like to meet someone WITH WHOM I need not share my knickers.

CLO: *Apocalypse Now!* I don't want to think about your knickers — OK, so I do, but not in front of my sister.

PERDITA: You are gross.

CLO: Zel gets me, don't you, Zel? He didn't exactly come all this way for the Foo-oo-ood and the Wi-ine.

PERDITA: Are you my brother? Somebody tell me it's a mistake. He came because I invited him.

CLO: What? You invited him for the food and wine? Oh, pardon ME! Zel, Zel! Can you complete this sentence? 'I wish I had someone I could share a . . . ' Easy, now — there are ladies present.

ZEL: Book. For me it would be a book.

PERDITA: Me too. Book.

HollyPollyMolly ggigggled with six gs and turned away — as discreetly as triplets wearing pinkpurplejade can do — to give Perdita some space.

ZEL: What book?

PERDITA: I'm reading a book my dad gave me by some nineteenth-century guy named Thoreau.

'*Walden?* You're reading *Walden?*'

'Yes! You know it?'

'My dad was always trying to get me to read it — which was pretty stupid as I wasn't even talking to him.'

'It's about only doing enough work to make enough money to live simply so that you can live in a more meaningful way.'

'Yeah. My dad tried that — a long time ago, when he was, like, our age. He lived in a van,

180

drove round to festivals, had no possessions.'

'Does he still do that?'

'No. He's rich.'

They laughed, a little bit awkwardly, and Zel said, 'I'm not rich. I work in a garage. But I can fix your car.'

'What book would you give me — if you wanted to give me a book?' said Perdita.

Zel opened the palms of his hands and studied them. 'I read obscure things — I mean, *Walden* is pretty obscure — I never read it because of my dad, sorry — so right now I'm reading Benjamin Franklin's autobiography. The guy on the hundred-dollar bill? I mean, we spend the money and we don't know anything about the people on the bills. Benjamin Franklin said that if you have to choose between liberty and security, choose liberty.'

'I guess they didn't have world terrorism back then.'

'That's just a way of scaring us.'

'I don't agree. People get killed.'

'Yes, they do, but some guy with a bomb in a backpack — how often does that happen, and to how many people? But no work, no home, no healthcare, no hope — that's the everyday life of millions, billions of people. To me, that's the threat. And climate change is the threat. And war, and drought and famine . . . '

'OK — so we need security. A secure future.'

'No! We need to be free from corporate control that runs the world for the few and ruins it for the rest of us.'

Perdita watched his mouth as he talked. She

liked what he was saying. But he could have been saying Yogi Bear Eats Peanut-Butter Sandwiches. She lifted her hand, because her hand, all on its own, was going to touch his lips. Halfway there her brain noticed and she brushed back her hair from her eyes instead.

She said, trying to sound provocative and cool, 'So if you don't care about security — what are you afraid of?'

'Me?' (Zel sighed and looked at his palms.) 'I guess I'm afraid of not being like other people. No, that's not true. I'm not afraid of not being like other people. I'm afraid I won't find anybody who doesn't mind me not being like other people. I'm not ambitious for money or power. I want to find some real way to live.'

She looked at his eyelashes, long and dark. He looked at her skin, pale and freckled. He had grey eyes like a cat. Her eyes were brown with her brown hair falling into them. She was like a close-up too far away to touch, her eyes so serious and beautiful, watching him. They were both leaning forward now in a mirror of the other.

Burst of laughter from the table.

CLO: Last question. LAST QUESTION. Everybody! Sister! You first! 'If I could go forward in time I'd like to be with . . .

With you. With you. With you.

★ ★ ★

The band were tuning up. People had started arriving, getting drinks; there was laughter, happiness, old friends.

Shep had showered and changed into his Sunday suit and he was walking through the bar. *This is my life*, he thought. *Here, all around me, and it is good.*

The banjo started a tune.

Shep came over to the table. HollyPollyMolly said, 'What did you get for your birthday, Shep?'

Shep leaned forward, pressing his hands on the table. 'I got a fine son and a fine daughter. That's all I want — well, and maybe a song . . . Perdita — you gonna go up there and sing that favourite of mine? The boys are ready for some music.'

Perdita got up and stood on tiptoe and kissed her father. Then she zigzagged through the people towards the stage. The boys nodded and smiled at her. Tom on banjo. Bill on tall bass. Steve on horn. Ron on guitar. Joey on the snares and harmonica.

They were doing a cover of an old Bette Midler cover of an old Tom Waits song. The banjo came in with Perdita's voice like a far-off story.

'*Well, I'm leavin' my family, leavin' all my friends. My body's at home, but my heart's in the wind . . .* '

Shep was sitting at the table beside Clo, drinking a slim bourbon, listening to her, watching her.

Suppose he had made a different choice that

night? Would he have walked away and forgotten about her?

What would his life have been back then, now? And her life?

That night, storm and rain and the moon like a mandala when the clouds parted, it was the moon that made him know. The baby had lain like the visible corner of a folded map. Traced inside her, faded now, were parents she would never know and a life that had vanished. Alternative routes she wouldn't take. People she would never meet. The would-be-that-wouldn't-be.

Because her mother or her father, or both, had left the map of her folded on the table and left the room.

It was a map of discovery. There were no more North Poles or Atlantic Oceans or Americas. The moon had been visited. And the bottom of the sea.

But she was setting out with the blank sheet and compass of herself.

Unpathed waters. Undreamed shores.

★   ★   ★

The song ended. Then Perdita took the microphone and asked for quiet.

'My father, Shep — you all know him' (CHEERS AND APPLAUSE) ' — we're here to celebrate his birthday' (MORE CHEERS) 'and in a minute we'll sing 'Happy Birthday' to him. But first I want to say thank you to him myself — for being the best dad in the world.'

Shep stood up. The band started playing. HAPPY BIRTHDAY TO YOU.

Then they heard it.

Was it thunder?

Was it a roar?

Was it an invasion?

Was it the Apocalypse?

Everyone stood watching as the big delivery doors onto the garden were pulled open by something or someone on or from the other side.

Full-flood headbeams. Low-slung growl. Clutch-controlled presidential slow speed of light.

It was the DeLorean.

ZEL: Oh no!

CLO: Satan's ass!

SHEP: What the . . . ?

The up-stroke gull-wings of the DeLorean lifted. Autolycus appeared by the side of the car as if he had always been there. He was wearing tapered black trousers, a black fine-knit polo neck and a red vest.

He looks like the Devil come for his money, thought Zel.

Did I say I'd pay him? thought Clo.

Autolycus jumped up on a chair and held up his hands. 'I am just the delivery boy. Clo! Clo! Where are you?'

Clo got up from the table. Where was the cartoon blade sawing round his cartoon chair to drop his cartoon self into oblivion?

'Here's the son!' said Autolycus. 'Where is the father?'

Shep came through the crowd. Autolycus shook his hand over and over like a wind-up toy.

'What is this?' said Shep. 'You some kind of cabaret act?'

'I am some kind of angel. Bringing good news. Clo! Clo!'

Clo pulled Autolycus to one side. 'Did I sign — you sayin' I signed?'

Autolycus unfolded a piece of paper from his pocket — Clo thought the piece of paper was really and truly and actually smoking.

'Yeah, yeah, you signed — see these flames and hoofprints here? Just kidding. I take the Silverado and you take the DeLorean — great deal, kid!'

Clo straightened up, turned to his father and cleared his throat. 'Dad, yeah, Dad — happy birthday; this is your car.'

'My car?'

Autolycus jumped like a circus dog onto his chair. 'Ladies and gentlemen! Attention, please! Introducing . . . THE DELOREAN!'

Already some of the men were nodding and cheering. Autolycus smiled modestly as if he had just won Miss America. There were tears in his eyes.

'*Thank you. Thank you.* I can hear some of you remembering it now. *Back to the Future* — the movie. 1985. That's right!

'The DeLorean is NOT just a car — it's a Time Machine.

'What did the great writer William Faulkner say?

'*"The past is not dead. It's not even past."*

186

(APPLAUSE)

Autolycus jumped down. 'Shep! Shep — get in the car! Guy who designed these — John DeLorean — he was six foot four. It's a big-guy car — that's why I had to sell it — trouble reaching the pedals — your son is truly a good son.'

★ ★ ★

VOICE IN THE CROWD: GO, GO, SHEP! GO BACK TO 1984 AND SAVE MARVIN GAYE!

★ ★ ★

Shep eased himself into the car and fired the engine.

Nothing happened. He tried again. Nothing. Autolycus looked a bit less easy — he pulled Clo aside. 'You got that hammer?'

Zel stopped running all of his hands through all of his hair and instead ran to the back of the DeLorean and opened it up.

'Zel! What are you doing here?'

'I TOLD you, I had a date — not that I will have a date now that you have fleeced the son and hijacked the dad's birthday.'

'Don't get mad at me.'

'Get out of the way!'

'You need a hammer?'

Zel took out his pocket Leatherman.

'That boy can fix anything — anything! Let me tell you how it is — cars like these are like racehorses.

'You want a car that GOES? Anybody can buy a car that GOES — it's almost vulgar. The DeLorean is not always a car that GOES but it is always a CAR. You know, let me tell you, when a car like this doesn't GO — it's really offering you a moment of Zen in a world obsessed with forward motion. Did you get your cortisol tested recently? America is running on cortisol. It's bad for your heart, bad for your cholesterol, bad for your marriage — snappy and yappy all the time. Now, when you jump into your car — this car — and you find you can't GO anywhere, that is a moment to ask yourself — where am I GOING?

'It's philosophy at your fingertips.

'This is a substantial car. Once you've driven — and also not driven — this car — a little bit Schrödinger's Cat, isn't it? Alive and dead at the same time — once you have had the DeLorean experience, the rest is just unconsidered trifles.'

Shep had his arms folded and was looking down at Autolycus — he was about a foot and a half taller than the persuasive trafficker of trifles.

'How much did my son pay for this philosophical car?'

'I pretty much gave it away. In honour of the occasion.'

'How much? Clo? Clo!'

At that second the DeLorean fired. Zel stood back from the engine, his white shirt oil-stained. His hands greased-up. The crowd cheered. Autolycus bowed.

'That's why we call cars 'she'. You never know. Remember that Billy Joel song? '*She's frequently kind and she's suddenly cruel. She can do as she pleases, she's nobody's fool.''*

'Does the mechanic come with the car?' said Shep.

Autolycus's pointy face brightened up. 'He's dating your daughter. So . . . '

'He's what?'

''*She's always a woman to me.*''

Shep looked from Zel to Autolycus and from Autolycus to Zel. 'Can you stop singing and can somebody tell me what any of this is about?'

'I am not dating your daughter.'

'Let's get a drink!' said Autolycus. 'A bourbon is halfway towards the truth any night of the week. Nice place you got here, Shep. You play poker?'

★   ★   ★

It was Perdita who found Zel, standing by the fence, angry and alone. She touched his back. He twitched like she'd poured water down his neck. He didn't turn round.

'I'm sorry,' he said.

'It's funny,' said Perdita.

Zel turned round. She was laughing. She was so pretty. Beyond her, the party was going on. People were playing with the DeLorean. The hum was easy, happy.

Zel so often put himself outside of where he wanted to be and then looked in dumbly through the window of his longing, hurt and beaten and knowing that he had hurt and beaten himself but still he did it, over and over.

Why was she comforting him? He should be the one comforting her. She had rowed out to reach him on his lonely island. She wanted to row him back with her to the lights and the warmth.

'Would you like to dance?'

He wanted to say 'I can't dance', but already she had taken his hand and was leading him towards the warm lights.

HollyPollyMolly, singing their close harmonies into the microphone, saw Perdita leading Zel through the crowded room towards the raised stage, where there was some space. Right then they were doing a Buddy Holly number that Shep liked, but Zel was never going to manage a jive — and besides, the triplets knew that Perdita needed to manage something else.

Holly pulled out of the sound for a second and said something to Bill on tall bass. He passed it on to the guys.

The music stopped, and before anyone could clap or pause the girls had started again with their own version of James Taylor's 'How Sweet It Is (To Be Loved By You)'.

Perdita took hold of Zel and guided him into something like dancing with her. He realised he was enjoying it.

'Do you ever walk in the rain just for the pleasure of getting wet?'

Zel smiled his slow, awkward, full-face smile like the sun coming through the clouds. He didn't reply. Instead he asked her a question.

'Do you get up sometimes or not go to bed sometimes, so that you can go for a walk without meeting anyone else at all?'

She said: Do you talk to yourself?

He said: Would you rather die well than live badly?

She said: Do you like stars?

He said: Do you like the ocean?

She said: Is this our own set of thirty-six questions?

He said: To fall in love?

No, she thought, *that's already happened, hasn't it?*

She said: To get to know each other?

He said: My dad spent a lot of time talking to psychologists about human behaviour — he needed the pre-sets.

Are there pre-sets?

Oh, yeah — most people will behave exactly as they are predicted to behave in any given situation.

What does he do, your dad?

He designs computer games. Not shoot-outs and trolls — sophisticated stuff.

Do you live with your mom and dad?

No. My mom and he never lived together — it's a long story, he's basically gay — him and my mom made an arrangement. He wanted a son. I was a vanity project.

Zel said this with such fierceness that Perdita wished she hadn't asked. She rubbed his shoulder. He didn't seem to notice her concern or her touch. He had left the present tense.

Dad was around a lot until I was about eight years old. Then he had some kind of a breakdown and after that we never saw him much. He paid all the bills. He paid for me to go to college.

As a mechanic?

No. I'm a Philosophy major. Does that surprise you?

Maybe . . . I don't know you.

But you do, he thought, coming back into the present. *You know me.*

Are you in touch with your dad?

Zel shook his head. 'He travels a lot. Also, he's a recluse — if you can be a recluse who travels a lot. Also, he's an alcoholic. So when I do see him I don't know if he will be drunk or sober. Usually he's so drunk he seems sober. That's the worst.'

'Is that why you don't drink? You always ask for water.'

Zel stood blank like metal. 'Can we talk about something else?'

Perdita moved her body against Zel, guiding his body with her body. He felt the warm softness of her right through him.

'I think I'm getting oil on your dress.'

They both looked down. GOD! HER BREASTS! Zel's body doing the thinking for him. He tried to focus his mind on disasters and drowning. Sick kittens. Laboratory chimps. Why had he worn tight jeans?

'Will you excuse me? I need the rest-room.'

★ ★ ★

HollyPollyMolly saw Zel dodge off as they came to the end of their set. Holly sat on the edge of the stage and grabbed Perdita.

'So? So SO SO SO SO???'

'So what?'

'You like him, don't you?'

'He's so serious and sweet.'

'And LOOK what he did to that car! Good with his hands.'

'Can you leave me alone? I love you but can you leave me alone? I'm getting some food.'

Perdita went over to the laden trestle. The chef was turning spring onions and prawns in a wok.

She took two servings and found a table. A little way off she could see her father playing cards with Autolycus and a man she didn't recognise.

Zel came back to the table. He had no bulges. Perdita pushed a plate of food over to him and grinned. He liked that; a girl who eats and a girl who grins. Nothing about her was self-conscious.

'Do you think you have any control over your life?' she said.

Zel thought this was a difficult question judging from his trip to the rest-room. He had been about to tell her that he liked her dress. Perdita was eating gracefully and messily — he wasn't sure how this combined but even the noodles she dropped she dropped elegantly.

Just do it forever, he thought, *do what you do forever. And let me be there.*

He said, 'Depends on whether you believe in free will or destiny. Let me see your hands — both of them; I'll come sit beside you.'

It was a good excuse to feel the strong length of her thigh against the strong length of his thigh.

'Can you read palms?'

'My mom can — her ancestors were slaves on the plantations; the knowledge was passed down the female line generation to generation. She's a little bit voodoo.'

Perdita gave him her left hand. Zel ran his finger around her palm. 'This is a map made of skin. You see this track, running down to your wrist — that's your life-line. And that's strange.'

'What? What's strange?'

'At the start of the line — here — there's a break, do you see? A complete break — like you were dead, but obviously you're not dead. And here, there's another line, like another life, shadowing the real one — and it joins your main-line here, like a disused railtrack.'

'That is my other life,' said Perdita. 'I'm adopted.'

'Oh . . . I'm sorry — forgive me, I didn't . . . '

'There's nothing to be sorry about. I'm adopted. So what?'

'Would you ever want to find your real parents?'

'In what sense would they be my parents? I mean, is a parent the person who provides you with the raw materials of life or the person who raises you? I love Shep. He's the one who's my father.'

Zel nodded. 'My dad's my dad, but I don't know him. He could be anybody's dad. I could be anybody's son.'

'What about your mom?'

'She's fine. She did her best.'

'My birth mother is dead. That's why I had to be adopted.'

'I'm so sorry.'

'Can you stop saying sorry?'

She put her finger on his lips. Then she leaned forward and kissed Zel. He wasn't the first boy she had kissed but he felt like it. He tasted of prawns and lime. He touched her hair gently as if she slept and he didn't want to wake her. He didn't want this dream to end.

★　★　★

Sometimes it doesn't matter that there was any time before this time. Sometimes it doesn't matter that it's night or day or now or then. Sometimes where you are is enough. It's not that time stops or that it hasn't started. This is time. You are here. This caught moment opening into a lifetime.

★　★　★

'I'm glad to see you young folks having such a good time,' said Autolycus, arriving at their table and sitting himself down.

Perdita looked across to Shep, who was still playing cards. Autolycus shook his head ruefully. 'That pop of yours is a sharp player. I'm out.'

'What did you lose this time?' said Zel.

'You sound like my mother. Don't worry about it. Life's a game of chance. Are you going to introduce me?'

'I'm Perdita.'

'A pleasure to meet you, Perdita. I'm Autolycus. Zel's told me all about you.'

'No, I haven't! I told you nothing about her.'

'That's how I knew you were serious.'

'We were talking about free will,' said Perdita. 'Do you believe in free will?'

'In theory I do, but they invented that idea before they invented the idea that makes free will an impossibility — like sex.'

'What's impossible about sex?'

'You're too young to know — let's stick with the topic.'

'You're the one who started talking about sex.'

'That's what happens when an old man sits next to a pretty young girl — but don't worry about it.'

'She won't,' said Zel.

'Thanks, I can speak for myself,' said Perdita.

Autolycus was nodding his head like a Chinese cat. 'That's right! I like a woman who speaks for herself! To get back to the topic — I can tell you that in my opinion the free market makes free will impossible.

'If I have to trade with you — Perdita — at a discount disadvantageous to me, where's my free will? And if I have to buy from you — Zel — because you're a monopoly pretending to be private enterprise, then where's my free will?'

Perdita said, 'Dad gave me *Walden* to read, that book by Thoreau? You can opt out of the system. You can live in your own way.'

Autolycus shrugged. 'What was that thing Jesus didn't say? The rich are always with you.

Drop out of the world and find an island where you can live on lettuce, and some venture capitalist will back a sea-plane shuttle service and they'll build a spa that offers a detox using only the world's most exclusive lettuce.'

'Aren't you a businessman?' said Perdita.

Autolycus shook his head. 'I'm too honest to be a businessman. I'm a straightforward crook.'

Shep came over to the table with a tall man Perdita didn't know.

'You want to jump back in for a last round?' Shep asked Autolycus.

'How much more can a poor old man risk?'

The stranger standing behind Zel spoke. 'What you risk reveals what you value.'

Zel turned round and stood up in the same moment. The softness in his face froze over like he was staring at Medusa.

'*Dad!*'

'Hello, Zel. Autolycus told me you would be here. I dropped in to pick up a car and I decided to come with him. I don't want to interrupt. I haven't seen you for a while.'

'Fourteen months,' said Zel. He was shaking with anger and confusion and he hoped no one could tell. It was always like this when he saw his father. His body went tense, his mind went blank and, while his father would be urbane and easy, Zel would have nothing to say. *Go away. Go away. Go away.*

Xeno looked Zel up and down like he was booking a model.

'You look good — apart from the oil-spill down your shirt.'

Zel blushed. He wanted to hit his father out of existence.

Xeno smiled at Perdita. He was taller than his son. Fine features and grey eyes. Thick grey hair combed back like a movie star's. Attractive and aware that he was attractive. He wore a dark blue tailored suit, lace-up blue suede Oxford brogues and a pink V-neck T-shirt. He held out his hand to Perdita.

'I'm Xeno. Zel's father.'

'You sound British,' said Perdita.

'I am British. Zel's American because his mother is American. And he was brought up here.'

'Perdita,' said Perdita. She took his hand to shake it. Xeno held on. Zel wished he had a knife.

The band started up a Jackson Browne number.

'People stay just a little bit longer . . . '

Xeno said, ''STAY'. This is one of my favourite songs from a long time ago. A lifetime ago. Before you were born. Would you like to dance?'

Perdita hesitated, then smiled and nodded and went with Xeno onto the dance floor.

Zel looked like he had been sprayed with ice-water and put in the fridge. He couldn't move and he didn't speak.

'Well, well,' said Autolycus. 'Family life is always a surprise.'

'He's not my family,' said Zel.

★   ★   ★

Xeno was a good dancer.

He moves like he's made of water, thought Perdita.

He didn't try to talk to her. They just danced in the way that people who can dance do dance.

He had the same slow, shy smile as Zel, but his face had an interiority to it that Zel's didn't. He seemed to be somewhere else, though not through inattentiveness; there was a quality of detachment to him.

Other dancers cleared a space around them because they were good to watch. Perdita was enjoying herself. Xeno got behind, letting her shimmy as he held her arms. He leaned forward and said into her ear, 'You're perfectly safe with me. I'm gay.'

Outside, on the edge of the dance floor, where he always felt himself to be, Zel was watching them. He stood, a motionless column of misery that couldn't be managed, and a rod of anger he couldn't express. He didn't want Xeno dancing with Perdita. At the same time he wanted his father to be dancing with him, on some other dance floor, where he had a father, and where his father had a son.

Perdita was aware of a doubleness in Xeno. His upper body was accommodating and polite. He twirled her, held out his hand to her, danced back, not forward — but his hips were forward water.

He was yes and no all at once.

The music ended. Xeno put his hand on the small of Perdita's back and indicated the direction of the bar. He asked for a double

199

Woodford Reserve. The barman didn't ask Perdita what she wanted — just passed her fresh lime juice and water.

Xeno dropped the bourbon down his throat like he was swallowing an oyster.

'How long have you known my son?'

'Not long. He comes to the bar sometimes.'

'I used to come here myself — years ago — before your family took it on. In those days this place had a reputation.'

'What kind of a reputation?'

'It doesn't matter. Times change. Or we believe that they do. But if times change, do people change?'

'I don't know what you mean . . .'

'That doesn't matter either. It's a long story. I think about time all the time — and in part because I am getting older. Don't mistake me — I am not wistful for lost youth. There's nothing there I want back. Not the van, the dog, the books, the girls, the boys, or Leo.'

'Who's Leo?'

'A lion I used to know.'

Perdita had a sense that Xeno's grey eyes, the colour of magnets, were magnets. He held her without touching her.

'I think about time because I don't understand it — we're the same there, you and I — except that you don't need to understand because you don't believe it will end. Don't you find that strange? That we think we're immortal until we're not?'

The barman came by and filled Xeno's glass. He lifted a toast to Perdita and drank back the whisky like he was Tristan and she was Isolde.

He said, 'Getting older happens suddenly. It's like swimming out to sea and realising that the shore you're making for isn't the shore where you started out.'

'Where did you start out?'

'At a chilly boys' boarding school in England. I liked swimming because the water was so cold that it stopped me feeling anything else.'

'I feel like I'm made of feelings.'

Xeno smiled at her. There was something about her that he thought he knew. But that was impossible.

He lifted his hand — he had easy, natural authority. The barman refilled his glass.

'Do you like him? Zel?'

'Yes, I do.'

Xeno nodded.

Then she said, 'Do you?'

Xeno downed his drink. He put his hand on her shoulder and they went back to the table.

Zel wasn't there. Clo was looking like that cat who got the cream, the kippers, the peanut butter, the sliced chicken and a lifetime's supply of genetically engineered slow-moving mice.

'Hey hey hey!' he said. 'Hey! Who wants a game?'

He was magician-trick shuffling the deck of cards one hand to the other, back and forth, like they were the leather pleats of a piano accordion.

'I won back the Chevy,' said Clo.

'Excuse me?' said Shep, who had won back the Chevy.

There was a family-sized bottle of Maker's

Mark on the table and a pitcher of ice and a round of glasses. Xeno poured a long straight bourbon into his glass — so much bourbon that he might have been a maiden aunt sitting with an iced tea.

'Help yourself,' said Shep.

'I already lost large,' said Xeno. 'I need a drink.'

'It's my birthday,' said Shep. 'I'm lucky tonight.'

'Or does the House always win?' said Xeno, dropping the whisky in one and pouring himself another long straight.

'There is no House,' said Shep. 'This isn't a laundromat.'

'It's a long way to drive for a drink.'

Shep cut the cards. 'Are you in or are you out?'

'I'm in,' said Xeno. 'I'll raise you large or quits.' He threw a thousand dollars onto the table.

'Holy Ghost and all the Saints,' said Clo.

'OK, OK,' said Autolycus, 'I'm in. Lowball or Texas Hold 'em?'

'I'm out,' said Clo.

'Can I play?' said Perdita.

'Since when did you learn how to play poker?' said Clo.

'Tonight. Teach me. Can we start with ten dollars?'

The men laughed. The moment lifted. 'We can play a junior game,' said Shep. 'Starter for ten, gentlemen.'

Xeno looked at Perdita. 'Poker is about

probability. You could say that poker-players are searching for order in a disordered universe.'

'Oh, I agree,' said Autolycus. 'Order/disorder. Disorder/ order. Can I get some whisky on this ice?'

Xeno continued. 'No one can predict the hand they are dealt, but because there are fifty-two cards in the pack you can soon work out what other people are playing. If you pay attention. So pay attention.'

'Let me explain how you play in real life,' said Shep, 'separate to all this philosophising — I got enough of that in the DeLorean.'

'There's no need to be hurtful,' said Autolycus.

Shep ignored him. 'Poker is a five-card game. This game, you got two hole cards — personal cards — and there's five community cards — like this — and here's what kinda hands you need to win. A hand is always five cards. You got your Royal Flush, your Straight Flush, Pairs . . . '

Zel came back to the table. His shirt was dripping wet but the oil had gone.

'My son seems to have laundered himself,' said Xeno. 'Is that what happens here?'

'Are you trying to say something?' said Shep.

'He's drunk,' said Zel. 'He's always drunk.'

Xeno refilled his glass, looking steadily at his son. 'All I'm saying is that this used to be a Mafia place.'

'Not any more,' said Shep.

Perdita took Zel's hand. 'I'm learning to play poker. Will you play?'

Zel took ten dollars from his billfold.

'I didn't know you knew how to play poker,' said Xeno.

'What do you know about me?' said Zel.

'Gentlemen . . . ' said Autolycus. 'We are guests at a party.'

'Uninvited guests,' said Shep, 'but, as it says in the Good Book, 'Be not inhospitable to strangers, lest they be angels in disguise.''

'I thought that was W. B. Yeats,' said Xeno.

'If it is, we know where he got it from,' said Shep.

'This is a funny kinda poker game,' said Autolycus. 'I should have stayed home. Clo! Put your bills on the table. You got plenty of money to spare thanks to the misfortune of an old man.'

Shep dealt the cards. It was a slow game, because the game was more than the cards. Xeno was drinking, Zel was hating, Shep was thinking, Autolycus was watching, Clo was being Clo, which was the same as being a table or a chair, and Perdita was learning.

She won the first hand. The men clapped.

'OK!' she said. 'Here's my fifty I won. Double or quits.'

Zel was the first to put fifty on the table.

'I pay that boy too much,' said Autolycus.

'Don't worry about him. He gets money from me every month,' said Xeno.

'I don't need your money. Why is it always about money with you?'

'I used to deal in other currencies,' said Xeno, 'love, friendship, trust, loyalty. And I felt good about myself. And then I discovered that it's all sentiment. Means nothing. We don't love others and others don't love us.'

'That's not true,' said Perdita.

'You're young,' said Xeno, 'you still believe in love.'

'That's because she is loved,' said Shep.

'And when she isn't? Read Oscar Wilde, my dear. Each man kills the thing he loves.'

'Why did you come here?' said Zel.

'I wanted to see you.'

'Then why didn't you? You have had years to see me.'

Xeno didn't answer.

'All right, all right,' said Shep. 'We're starting the game.'

Xeno put down the cash. He didn't look at Zel.

This time the men were playing for real.

Perdita won the second hand. She scooped up the $250 and added her own stake. $300 to play.

'I'm out,' said Zel.

'I'll stake you,' said Xeno.

'I said I'm out.'

'I said I'll stake you!'

'I'm out,' said Clo.

'You're in,' said Shep. 'Put the money on the table and do as you're told.'

Autolycus said, 'Clo — you know that story I told you this morning, about Oedipus?'

'Yeah, yeah,' said Clo. 'What about it?'

'I am revising my thesis. It's the fathers who kill the sons.'

'Who kills the daughters?' said Perdita.

'We all do,' said Xeno. 'If the hero doesn't kill you — call him Hamlet, call him Othello, call him Leontes, Don Giovanni, James Bond — still you'll be the sacrifice for his soul.'

'Does everyone except me know what he's talking about?' said Clo.

'When he's drunk,' said Zel, 'he thinks he's interesting.'

Xeno said, 'My best friend once bet me his wife.'

'Did you play?' said Shep.

'No. But we both lost.'

★ ★ ★

There was $4000 on the table. Autolycus played his hand. Straight Flush.

'Thank you, Gentlemen, and this dear lady.'

'Well, well, well, well, abide with me,' said Shep.

'Better quit while I'm ahead.' Autolycus stood up, folding the cash into his wallet.

'You dropped this.' Perdita handed him a playing card from his chair.

Shep took it from her. 'That's not from our pack.'

Xeno leaned back, his hands behind his head. 'The biter bit. The House doesn't like cheating unless it's the House that cheats.'

Shep turned on Xeno. 'This is not a House.'

'Oh, no? What are you running out here, Shep? Drugs? Women? Underage girls? Boys? No, it's not boys or I'd have heard about it.'

'Have you lost your mind?' said Zel.

'I think it's time for you to leave,' said Shep.

Xeno didn't move. His long fingers were like

spider legs, Perdita thought as he played them up and down his tumbler of bourbon like a spider crawling up and down the glass.

Xeno said, 'This was a Mafia place when you took it over. I was more involved in the city at that time. I was living here at that time. I know some things.'

Shep was working hard to control his anger. 'Yes, it was a Mafia place. I bought them out.'

'No one buys the Mafia out.'

'That's true,' said Autolycus.

'You shut it,' said Clo. 'Perdita — you want to leave us for a while?'

'No.'

'I'm saying leave us for a while.'

'You don't want her to hear how her father runs his business? You don't buy your daughter a necklace like the one she's wearing out of cash from bowls of fish soup and Friday night Golden Oldies.'

'This was my mother's necklace,' said Perdita.

'Her mother's dead,' said Zel. 'You are crass, drunk, self-obsessed and stupid.'

Clo stood up. He was as tall as his father with double the bulk. 'Time's up, Beano, or whatever you call yourself. You're lucky. If this was a Mafia place, you'd have a bullet in your head by morning.'

'Like Tony Gonzales,' said Xeno.

Silence.

'Tony . . . Gonzales . . . ' said Autolycus. 'Whew-whee. That was a long time ago.'

'Who's Tony Gonzales?'

'It was before you were born,' said Autolycus.

'*Before she was born*,' repeated Shep, his speech slow.

'I bought the scrap, y'know, piece of local history.'

'What scrap?' said Clo.

'Whoever shot that guy — and they never caught them, right?'

'They were never caught,' said Xeno.

'They made off in the Mexican's rented BMW and they rear-ended that car under Bear Bridge. The floodwater that night was like God had sent it.'

'*Like God had sent it*,' repeated Shep, his speech slow and automatic.

'I got the call to come and collect the wreck — I was doing mostly wreck work in those days. To pay the bills. The pistol they shot the Mexican with — it was still in the car when I got there; police never worked out why there was one bullet they couldn't account for. Six to a barrel, two in the Mexican, three in the gun.'

'They must'a fired and missed,' said Clo.

'Yeah, maybe. There was a witness — a medical orderly — coming out of the hospital, said he'd seen a car with a blown-out tyre and a couple of guys changing the wheel in the rain like some drenched film noir. But they never found them either. Lordy, yes, it's coming back to me now. It was in the news for quite a few weeks.'

Xeno emptied the rest of the bottle into his glass.

'I was the man Tony Gonzales was looking for.'

Silence.

'That guy was bringing YOU the money and the . . . ?' Clo had started speaking and then he stopped speaking. Shep was on his feet. He was swaying slightly. His face was twitching and he seemed to be trying to say something that wouldn't be said and trying to walk away from the table that stayed where it was or his body stayed where it was. He was moving and speaking/not moving/not speaking.

'Dad?'

Shep fell like a falling world.

'Dad? Dad!'

Clo was gently slapping his face. People were gathering round. 'Get an ambulance! GET AN AMBULANCE!'

★   ★   ★

And the night unwound as those days and nights do — those days and nights that hijack time. Those days and nights that hold up the car on its way home and gun down the driver and the passengers and leave the wreckage in the rain.

You were moving through your days and nights and then the call came. You were thinking about supper or going to bed. You weren't thinking about death and loss. And now there's a flood and it's dark and you're trying to get there before it's too late but it's already too late because the time where there was enough time is over. You don't know how long it is until morning and in the hospital the hands on the clock crawl round like an insect walking the same pane of glass till it dies.

The rubber tube on his finger attaches to the heart monitor. The mask over his face gives him oxygen from a bottle. His eyes are closed. He still looks like himself but his eyes are closed. Then they came to wheel the bed along the Lino corridor and down to the basement for an MRI scan and it was all in a night's work to them and they would go home and sleep, but not you.

What did they write over the bed in wipe-away marker pen? The name of the doctor in charge and the time of admission and Nil by Mouth. It sounded like an island far away.

Where have you gone?

She bent over him and kissed him. Mouth to mouth. His lips were dry and salty and unresponsive. This wasn't a fairy tale. Love couldn't rouse him.

Two hard vinyl-covered chairs shoved together seat to seat. A thin blue blanket that smelt of Dettol. Sleep beside the high white bed and its metal safety rails. Sleep under the flickering monitor of his life. Beyond the capsule of the room are the bright lights of the nurses' station and the neon busyness of hospital nights. But in here there's the low lamp that lights his face and the green, red and blue of the monitor and outside through the window the heads and tails of hundreds of cars, all going home, not like you. Still part of time. Not like you.

The long watches of the night.

★ ★ ★

210

I love you and there is nothing I can do.

★ ★ ★

Clo was sitting blankly in front of the blank TV screen when Perdita came home from the hospital. They were doing more tests. They had told her to go home and get some rest.

She went to her little room where the sun made diamonds on the clean, bare floor. Everything seemed the same and nothing was the same. The illusion of objects.

She slept fitfully at first and then deeply. It was already evening when she woke. She showered and changed, jeans and a sweatshirt, and went downstairs.

Clo was clearing up from the night before. He saw her and smiled. 'You want food? We got a heap of shrimp left over so I made chowder.'

They sat together in silence at the table. Clo kept glancing at her as he ate. She hadn't eaten all day and she was hungry. When she had finished she looked straight at him. He looked away.

'Clo? There's things I don't know, aren't there?'

'Ask Dad.'

'I can't ask Dad. Whatever happened last night — Dad had a stroke and now he's in hospital. What did happen?'

'I'm not up to this.'

'Just tell me.'

'Dad was gonna tell you when you turned eighteen.'

'I need to know!'

Clo stood up slowly, pushing from his thighs like a man lifting a weight. 'Give me a minute, OK?'

He left the room while Perdita cleared the dishes. She dropped a bowl and broke it. She bent to pick up the pieces and knocked a glass off the table.

Clo came back in with a big square attaché case and a cardboard box file.

'Let me do the dishes. It'll be cheaper.'

He grinned at her, trying to help her, but she was staring at the case, not at him. He let out a big all-of-his-mouth blown-out-cheeks sigh and put the case on the table.

Perdita felt fear. Fear of the tarnished snaplocks. Fear of the dull, unused leather.

Clo started with the box file. Inside were newspaper clippings, internet downloads, grainy pictures of darkness and flood.

'I put these together at the time and for a few months afterwards. I was waiting to get arrested.'

Perdita turned over the clippings. Bridges, police cars, weather reports, breaking news, broken lives.

'Did you — did Dad — kill . . . ?'

'NO! Do I look like a murderer? No. We tried to help that Gonzales guy. We were driving. Trying to get home. We saw the car-jack. We went to help him. But it was too late. He hit his head when he fell. I have to say we didn't know he had been shot. In fact I don't know that he had been shot. But he was dead.

'Dad wouldn't wait for the cops. You know he

doesn't trust the cops. He thought they'd frame us. We're black, for Christ's sake.'

Perdita was turning over the clippings.

'You were the men the cops were looking for?'

Clo nodded; his hand was gripping the table. 'Holy of holies, was I scared. We were the unidentified guys in the unidentified car.'

★ ★ ★

It was a week or so after the homicide that the TV news started the hunt for a baby that had travelled with Tony Gonzales from London. Gone missing were half a million dollars and a baby girl known only as Baby M.

> *Police understand from the parents of the child that Baby M was to be delivered to a close friend of the family who has not yet been traced.*
>
> *A hospital nurse, Anna Conchitas, confirmed that Mr Gonzales had brought the baby into Sainta Maria Hospital in the early hours of Sunday morning and that the baby was in good health and there was nothing irregular. Mrs Conchitas was the last person to see either Mr Gonzales or Baby M. Police confirmed that formula milk and diapers were in the back seat of the car. Mr Gonzales had left his luggage at the hotel, an indication that he had intended to return there.*

★ ★ ★

'Yeah, that was the report. I never showed it to Dad. I don't know how much he really knew. He wouldn't watch the news. He wouldn't talk about anything. Once he had made up his mind to hold on to you he didn't want to know anything else. He kept you hidden away in the apartment for a couple of months. Then we moved out to a rental in the suburbs. Folks assumed the kid was mine — another black guy without a job and with a kid — and that Shep was the church-going grandfather trying to do the right thing. Pious white folks beating the shit out of each other with the curtains closed and looking down on black families — all that stuff.

'Then he bought this place.'

'With the money?'

'Yeah, with the money in the case and with the sale of his apartment. We had a good apartment. My mom had an insurance policy — paid out when she died and cleared the loans.'

'What did Xeno mean about the Mafia?'

'He was full of drink and shit. We aren't Mafia! You ever seen any Mafia types round here? No!'

'Was I in the car?'

'No, you wasn't in the car. The guy Gonzales must'a known there was trouble. He stowed you away — we reckon he was coming back for you.'

'Where was I?'

Clo looked uncomfortable. 'We pulled round to the hospital to fix the tyre and get out of the way, and while I was doing it — couldn't see my own fingers through the rain — Dad saw you.'

'WHERE?'

'The hospital used to have a BabyHatch — for babies . . .'

'Like HollyPollyMolly in Guangzhou?'

'Just the same. Are you OK?'

Perdita had sat down. 'Just keep talking,' she said, because she feared that if he stopped he wouldn't have the courage to start again and she wouldn't have the courage to hear him.

'The BabyHatch was there a few years. Then the moral majority, whoever they are, got it taken away. Never mind that. Dad knew from the start the crazy mess was connected — the baby — that was you — the businessman, the car-jack — but he didn't know how.

'He had a hunch. I thought he was crazy. Turned out he wasn't crazy. But it was maybe two weeks later that more of the story started coming out.

'That Xeno guy — they found him — he was in Paris. I didn't recognise him last night — it was only a photo I saw, and it was a long time ago. It's in here somewhere. He had some kind of long foreign name — Polixenes, or Polixeno — Greek or Brazilian or Argentinian maybe, and dark hair and a beard . . . you want to find the photo?'

Perdita shook her head. 'Not now.'

'That's when we shudda marched down to the NBPD and handed you back, and the money too. The money was in there with you — in this briefcase right here.'

Clo's big thumbs clicked the snaplocks. The case lid opened at the hinges.

'Go ahead — look inside.'

215

Inside were ten hundred-dollar bills.

'Look at that! I guess Dad must have left them for you to see. It was all bills like that. Yeah. Stacked up like in a movie. And the jewels. Like a fairy tale.'

'Why didn't you go to the cops — was it for the cash?'

'No! It was for you! I never seen a man so fallen in love as Dad was with you. Dad said — his reasoning was — if they had given you away, why were we giving you back? He thought you might get sent to an orphanage. He believed that God had given you to him. And who is to say that ain't so?'

Perdita picked up the bills like they were letters to her.

'And I was scared that we were in trouble by then. So we legally registered you — we found a woman who wanted money and she agreed to name herself as your mother and Shep as your father. She didn't know nothing. She didn't care. It was about money to her. We changed your birth date. That's how you got a passport, birth certificate, social security, all the shit.'

'How old am I?'

'Around three months older than you are.'

*　*　*

Perdita sat down on the couch. Clo came and sat with her and put his arm around her. 'You're still my little sister.'

'Am I?'

'Too bad, yeah — you'll always be my sister.

216

Listen to me. I'm not smart, you know that.' He nudged her. 'Go on, you can be honest — this is a day for honesty. OK, I'm a few neons short of a light show.'

Perdita was laughing as well as crying. Clo held her tight against his big shoulder and chest. He smelled of soap and cologne.

'But I see what's plain to see. Unhappy families every place. The dad walks out or the mom's on pills or cheating. The kids hate everybody and leave home as soon as they can feed themselves. We're your family because we want to be. If they had'a found Dad they would'a arrested him. That's how much he wanted you.'

Perdita wiped her face on Clo's T-shirt.

'Will you drive me down to the garage?'

'Autolycus's place? What for?'

'I want to see Zel.'

Clo looked uneasy but he went for his jacket and keys. In the car, with the radio on, and them both looking straight ahead, because it is easier sometimes to say things when you are both looking straight ahead, Clo said, 'You and Dad . . . I meant what I said. It was love at first sight, him and you. You know, you mended him.'

'Mended him?'

'After Mom died he had a broken heart. You mended his heart.'

Clo reached across and took her hand. They drove like that without speaking, each travelling through parts of their past, until the lights of the town slowed them down into the evening that was now.

Autolycus was polishing a car. He came straight up to Clo and shook his hand, putting his other hand on Perdita's shoulder. He didn't say anything. There was no need.

Zel slid out on a skateboard from the undercarriage of a black upright Model T Ford.

He spread out his hands, looking down as he spoke.

'I am sorry.'

Perdita said, 'I need to see Xeno.'

Time's News

The house was dark and set back from the road.

Under the moonlight, visible, a wisteria that had once been trained up the brickwork had long since grown across the iron balconies. Some of the windows were obscured. The paint on the front door had been softened and defeated by the hot, moist air. The wide, deep steps up to the door hadn't been swept in a long time.

It looked like a house in a story.

Zel unlocked the heavy gates that secured the entrance. They drove in across the gravel.

Does anyone live here?

He lives here.

★ ★ ★

Zel led Perdita round the side of the building. The brickwork was damp. The garden was overgrown. Nature versus Us. The constant effort of being human. The constant anxiety of being human.

Holding her hand, Zel took Perdita down some slippy shallow steps, cracked with ferns, descending into what was once the old kitchen. Now it was a lumber-room. He put his hand up inside a grating and drew out a big key like at the beginning of *Bluebeard*.

Zel pushed open the door. They heard scuttering.

'You scared of mice?' She isn't.

'Light's just here.' Click-click of a switch. Nothing.

Zel held Perdita's hand and took her haltingly, slowly, up a flight of narrow servants' stairs that led into a wide hall. He lifted his phone over his head, giving a thin, diffuse light. Perdita saw shadows and deep-recessed doors. A broad, imposing staircase. This house had been a grand house.

'Let's try the library,' said Zel, opening a pair of inlaid rosewood doors.

The air was stale and dusty. The shutters were closed. There were two big church candles on the stone mantelpiece. Zel lit them. That was better. At least they could see.

Perdita was shivering. The house was cold with the cold that comes when humans go away.

'I'll light a fire.'

Zel knelt down — everything was there that he needed, as though once, some time, someone had wanted to light a fire. Taken pleasure in split kindling and dry logs.

The big room had two walls lined floor-to-ceiling with books. Old books, expensive books — natural history, science, architecture, biography. In front of the dusty fireplace were two deep leather armchairs scuffed by time. 'He loves books,' said Perdita.

'Yeah. He does. When you've finished a book you can put it away and it doesn't ask to see you again.'

Perdita went over to the full-length window that was shuttered and barred. She swung the metal stay from its keep and let it drop half a circle so that she could open the shutter and bring in some light from the undarkened sky. At this time of the year the sky had light all night.

The shutters were well-oiled at the hinges and folded back into their boxes, original, in rosewood, from the colonial days of the house. Perdita ran her hand down the smooth wood, wondering how many hands had opened and closed these shutters: felt indifference or despair at another night, or happiness, because the day had come.

She liked old houses. Not having a history of her own, she was drawn towards the history of others.

'How old is this house?'

'It's French. So it's old.'

The fire had caught and the young flames filled the room with sudden light and the beginnings of warmth.

Perdita went and crouched down next to it.

'Why do you think he's here?'

'He's here.'

Zel came and knelt beside her. 'If I hadn't come to the bar none of this would have happened.'

'Something would have happened.'

'Now you sound like him.'

'Zel, think back — what did happen?'

Zel shook his head. 'I don't really recall. He was around, coming and going, but around, until I was about eight, I guess. Then we hardly saw him. He paid all the bills but he just wasn't there. Like he was dead. I had a dad and then I didn't have a dad.'

'Does that mean he ran out on you around the time of the murder and the money and the baby?'

Zel nodded. 'I suppose that's right. Mom never said anything — nothing at all. Then Mom and I moved to New York City.'

'Do you remember the murder? Last night, what they were saying? Tony Gonzales?'

'No. I was a kid. All I remember is that we were moving. I came back here in the holidays at first, for a couple of years, I think, and then the place started getting more and more run-down — no housekeeper, no maintenance. Then one day I arrived at the airport — I was about eleven — and he wasn't there to meet me. I waited at the airport all day — he didn't come. Finally I called Mom and she had them put me back on the last flight to New York.'

'What happened?'

'Nothing. I didn't see him again till I started college in St Louis. He bought me a motorcycle and taped a note to the seat that said, 'DON'T KILL YOURSELF. DAD.''

'Did he ever take you to England with him?'

'Yes. When I was a kid — before it went wrong. And they came to see us.'

'Who did?'

'His best friend — Uncle Lion. MiMi, that was his wife, and Milo — Milo was their son, same age as me. They all came here, to this house, and Mom and me came here, and twice I went to London, but I don't remember all that much about it. Why are you asking?'

Perdita said, 'I think you might be my brother.'

★　★　★

Zel was on his feet. He was running. He wasn't breathing. He was sweating. His chest hurt as if someone had thrown a brick at him. She was his new world not his old world. She was sight of land. She was the stretch and chance of time. And he had kissed her. And he wanted to go on kissing her. He hated his father.

★　★　★

Perdita came after him into the big, shadowy hall backlit from the fire and candles in the library. She heard his boots beyond the house running across the gravel. She didn't feel anything, in that moment, not fear, not sadness, not surprise, not the need to act. What she felt, or rather what she observed — because she had the curious sense that she was an avatar and that this was not her body — was a feeling of inevitability. It had come to this. It was coming to this. This was her coordinate in time.

★　★　★

And then the lights came on in the hall. The big, ten-bannered drop-down chandelier lit up like the start of a ball. Music. Upstairs.

'*Laugh about it, shout about it, when you've*

got to choose. Every way you look at this you lose . . . '

Perdita stood at the foot of the staircase with its wide mahogany treads, wide enough for three people to ascend together. The staircase divided right and left at the first landing, leading to wide passages on either side.

She went up to the first landing.

'It's a little secret, just the Robinsons' affair. Most of all you've got to hide it from the kids . . . '

Every door was open — bedrooms silent and unslept-in. To the left again there was a further staircase, shorter, narrower, to what must have been the servants' quarters once.

The music was loud now. The small door at the top of the stairs was open.

Perdita went and stood in the doorway.

★ ★ ★

The room was huge — an opened-out attic spanning the length and breadth of the house. The space was furnished in blues and pinks, with rugs, lamps, pictures, sofas. A vast apex skylight let in the stars.

A long, pale birchwood desk was banked with computer equipment. A screen filled one wall entirely.

★ ★ ★

Is that Paris?

It is Paris savaged by broken angels.

226

⋆   ⋆   ⋆

Xeno turned from the computer. He stood up.
He was wearing perfectly faded jeans and a new
white T-shirt. His feet were bare. There was a
bottle of Woodford Reserve on the desk. He
lifted it at Perdita, who shook her head. Xeno
poured for himself. 'How is your father?'

'Stable.'

Xeno nodded. She fascinated him. She had no
fear and he realised he was afraid of her.

'I'm here because I want to talk to you about
what you said last night.'

Xeno took a drink. 'I don't suppose you're a
gamer? Women aren't, usually. It's not brain-
wiring, it's because games are not designed with
women in mind — rather like cars, except for
small, silly under-powered cars. I never understood that.'

Xeno turned back to the screen and pressed
play. An avatar of himself stood in an empty
street, where it snowed feathers.

'What are you doing?'

'For now, collecting feathers. Do you want to
help me? Here.'

Xeno picked up his iPad and photographed
Perdita. He uploaded it. As he talked, her image
became an avatar and she entered the game.

'I design and code games. The usual ones:
crashes, explosions, trolls, cloaks, treasure. But I
try and do things differently too. Have you
noticed how ninety per cent of games feature
tattooed white men with buzzcuts beating the
shit out of the world in stolen cars? It's like living

227

in a hardcore gay nightclub on a military base.

'This game — 'The Gap of Time' — is my game. I started to build it a long time ago — before it happened.'

'Before what happened?'

'The end of the world.'

He was intense at the screen. She knew she must just let him talk, let him play, and try to understand. She thought he was crazy but if she didn't go along with the craziness she would never find out the truth.

'Do you speak French?' he said.

'No.'

Xeno swivelled round, stretching his long legs and flexing his toes. His toes were long like fingers and again she had the image of the spider, this time in a web hammocked across the house.

He took a drink.

'There was a French poet called Gérard de Nerval. Nineteenth-century. Just before he killed himself he had a dream that a fallen angel was trapped in the tiny courtyard behind the decaying houses where he lived. The space above the courtyard where the tall houses leaned in four-square was like a funnel with a cutting of sky at the top. The angel had landed on the lead pitch of the roof and slipped.

'Once the angel was trapped in the funnel he could not save himself because he could not open his wings to fly away.

'When the angel became trapped his head was level with the upper floors of the houses and a little child used to come and talk to him. She sat on the windowsill, her knees drawn up against the cold, and she told the angel stories her mother had told her, so many stories of lost and found, and the angel loved her.

'At night, sometimes, she'd bring a candle to the window and sit with the angel because she knew he was lonely.

'Weeks passed and the angel began to die. As he died he shrank, and the child went from window to window, zigzagging down the house, her small body by his great fallen head. She stroked his tarnished hair.

'At last, the feathers of his six wings began to separate from the bone and cartilage. The angel was dissolving into a pile of feathers. He called the child, with his voice that sounded like a trumpet, and the child came out of the back door into the midden courtyard. She sank into the feathers heaping like snow and the angel lifted her up with his last strength and put her just above him on the long window ledge.

' 'Take the diamond feathers,' he said. 'The two that wing across my collarbone.'

'The child didn't want to because she knew it would hurt him.

' 'Take them. Keep them. One is the Flight of Love. The other is the Flight of Time.'

'The child pulled at the diamond feathers but they held fast.

' 'Take your little knife and cut them where they bone,' said the angel. 'Look, I will turn my neck.'

'And the child took her little knife and cut the feathers where they boned. And the feathers shone in the snow. And the angel died.

'And there was a great rush of wind that filled the courtyard and the child had to cover her face and crouch in the reveal of the window or she would have been blown away. And every feather spun up into the cold blue air and blew over the city like birds.

'But the diamond feathers weren't flying-away feathers; they were solid as a promise that will be kept.

'Birds sing. Fish swim. Time passes. The little girl became a woman and went away.'

★ ★ ★

Said Xeno, 'Nerval didn't go beyond the trapped angel; that was his dream. My dream was the child and the promise. And at first the rest of my dream was pretty. I imagined a city where each of the flying-away feathers had become its own angel — because it would be nice to grow an angel from a feather. 'But then I saw that these angels are fallen. They are dark angels of death.

'The Angels want the city for themselves. To achieve that the city must become as necrotic as they are. The Angels turn man against woman, woman against child. There is no pity or justice, only fear and the pleasure of pain. This is the fallen world. Every day the city darkens.'

'There's no one out on the streets except us,' said Perdita.

'It will soon be curfew.'

'Why are we gathering feathers?'

'Feathers that fall on stony ground — roads,

streets, yards, bridges — can't grow. That's good. People use them for fuel and for bedding because the city is cold. But it is better to destroy them. You see, a feather that comes into contact with fire — including electricity — combusts. Those become the Angels of the Watch. Their wings have eyes.

'Any feather that comes into contact with water, swells. These become Sunken Angels. They are in the subways and sewers, the tunnels and shafts and undergrounds of Paris.

'The game has nine levels. At Level 4 you can move around in time. At any point in the game you can deepfreeze an action, an event, a happening and return to it later — because, perhaps, you can make it unhappen.

'I suppose that's what I wanted to do; make things unhappen.'

'What do you want me to do with this sack of feathers?' said Perdita.

'I have a friend who turns them into chickens. The city needs food. The city is divided into Resisters and Collaborators. It means something different here, to be on the side of the Angels.'

'Is this Level 1?'

'Level 1 is the Tragic Plane. Disastrous. Calamitous. Catastrophic. Dreadful. Ruinous. Wretched. Miserable. Terrible. Untruthful. Unfortunate. That would not make it tragic, though, would it? That's how life is. It is tragic because there is also glory, chance, optimism, bravery, sacrifice, struggle, hope, goodness. And all of that is embedded in the game.'

Perdita and Xeno walked through the falling

snow past a bookshop.

'Shakespeare and Company. They are Resisters. You can sleep there tonight. Or you can stay with me. My apartment is just round the corner. Underneath MiMi.'

'MiMi?'

'MiMi was Leo's wife.'

'You said you wanted to make it unhappen. What?'

'Did you ever watch Superman movies? Too young, I guess.'

He didn't wait for her to answer. 'My friend Leo loved that Superman movie where Lois Lane doesn't die in a car crash because Superman is powerful enough to belt the earth like Puck on speed and turn back time.'

'Who is Leo?'

'You asked me that already.'

'It's a different question now.'

'He nearly killed me twice. I couldn't risk it a third time.'

'Is he here?'

'In the game? Yes. We keep in touch that way. He's moving through the city now. I can sense him. He has a big following. He likes a crowd.'

'Is he collecting feathers?'

Xeno laughed. 'Leo? Do litter duty? No. But he wouldn't be doing that anyway. He's an Archangel.'

★   ★   ★

The cold, empty city is here and there lit up by bursts of flame. Men and women on the streets warming themselves at fires they have not lit and cannot put out. The Angels are the keepers of fire.

★ ★ ★

'Tell me what happened,' said Perdita.

'There was a child,' said Xeno. 'Leo was sure I was the father. He didn't believe me, or his wife, or the DNA test. DNA tests are ninety-nine per cent accurate but Leo liked to call himself the one per cent.'

'What did he do with the child?'

'He sent her to me but she never arrived.'

Perdita said, 'Were you the father?'

'No. Yes. Leo was the father. I loved them both. Leo and MiMi. I was in love with them both. And I always wanted a daughter.'

'Zel said you wanted a son.'

'He's my son. Yes, he is my son. And, strictly speaking, I am his father. And, strictly speaking, Leo was the baby's father. Those are facts but are they truths? What kind of a father have I been to Zel? The truth is I should have married MiMi. Me. Not Leo. Me. There was a moment — I really think she loved me, and I really think I loved her, enough to change everything, but he wanted her so much — and Leo gets what he wants — and I have never had a serious relationship with a woman, and I hesitate over what I want, and I thought I couldn't do it, and I thought, what did it matter? We will always be together, the three of us. I will love them both and I will be with them both. If they had wanted

233

it I would have been lovers with them both, too. Sometimes I think MiMi did want that.

'She trusted me. She was physically comfortable with me, maybe because there wasn't the erotic edge there was with Leo. Leo is confident and powerful — he's also an asshole — but he knows what he wants and he goes and gets it — that's attractive. I find it attractive. We were lovers once — when we were teenage boys. I don't know how real it was for him. But it was real for me.

'MiMi broke up with him — oh, for a year. I did nothing about it. And then he asked me to go and woo her back for him. He suddenly couldn't do it. I knew then he was serious, when his swagger and poise left him. So I went to woo her, and I think — no, I know — I still know, after all these years, that MiMi and I fell in love that weekend.

'I was a fucking coward.'

Xeno drank some more. Went to a sink in the corner of the room and spat it out. He turned to Perdita, wiping his mouth on his hand, and suddenly he didn't look urbane or in control. He looked like a tired, bloodshot drunk.

★ ★ ★

'He sent the baby to me and I wasn't there.

'Do you know what that means? I WASN'T THERE.'

Perdita sat still. Still like she was prey. Like she was prey with camouflage.

Xeno said, 'There's no need to lie any more.

What difference does it make? Because the past can't unhappen.

'The worst is hidden. You want it? You seem to want it. Here's the truth:

'I wasn't not there. I was there. I was here. In this house when Tony Gonzales came with the baby. Leo had emailed me. I didn't believe him. And then when it happened I thought Tony would just get on a plane and take the baby home and give her back to MiMi. I didn't know about the money. Leo did that to insult me. He could have wired it to my account and I would have wired it straight back, the asshole. But he put it in cash. It was a big bag of Fuck You.

'But someone did know about the money — there must have been a tip-off at the bank. It wasn't much money by criminal standards, but an easy heist from a hotel room, I guess. A pity to waste it. And it went wrong.'

'What did MiMi do?'

'MiMi? Come here. Look up.'

They walked round the corner of Saint-Julien-le-Pauvre. The tall, silent buildings were dark. Were they dark?

At the top was a small light in a small window.

'That's where MiMi lives. But she doesn't sing any more.'

'Not this MiMi — not the one in the game — the one in real life.'

Xeno said, 'If I could make it unhappen. And then I remember that the choices I made I made because there was no me to make any other choices. Free will depends on being stronger than the moment that traps you.

'It isn't fate. I don't believe in fate. Do you?'
He didn't wait for an answer.

'Our habits and our fears make our choices.
We are an algorithm of ourselves — *if you liked
that you may also like this.*'

Perdita said, 'Not the game, Xeno. In real life.
Is MiMi dead?'

Xeno said, 'Better ask me is she alive? No,
she's not alive in any way that makes being alive
a life. Shall I play you some of her music? Would
you like that?'

'She recorded music?'

'Here she is.'

'She's pregnant.'

'Yes. That was the night Leo nearly killed me
for the second time. That was the night the child
was born.'

'Does Leo live in London?'

'Yes. He's a reformed character. Quite the
angel. He invests money for children's charities
round the world. Let me Google him for you.
Voilà! Or *eccola!* His mother's Italian. Dad's
German. Leo looks like a German banker, acts
like an Italian Mafioso — fucking money in
fucking suitcases, running people down . . . Here
he is: 'SICILIA — BECAUSE LOVE COSTS
MONEY'. And underneath are all the projects
they've supported — schools built, wells dug,
scholarships provided, hospitals equipped. It's
impressive. But Leo is impressive. And I'll say
one thing for him, that sometimes makes me
believe his sorrow is sincere — he never married
again.'

Behind the huge wall-size photo of Leo that

Xeno had flipped up, MiMi went on singing — 'Is that man falling? Or is that man falling in love?'

Xeno said, 'Leo is addicted to drops — he dropped his entire life, and I was part of the fallout.'

'You are full of shit and self-pity,' said Zel.

Xeno turned from the wall-screen. 'Zel . . . I didn't see you.'

'Nothing different there,' said Zel.

'Zel, can we talk?' said Xeno.

'No, we can't. We can't because we don't and we don't because we can't.'

'Is that what they teach you in philosophy?'

'You always have to whip back, don't you? The smart hit?'

Xeno leaned on the edge of the desk. 'Zel, if I could change it . . . '

'It's not in the past,' said Perdita. 'You can't change what you did. You can change what you do.'

Xeno said, 'You sound like a fridge magnet.'

Zel said, 'You think you're a broken hero, don't you? But you're just a coward. You control life by avoiding it — relationships, children, people. You don't know how to love — that's all. You pretend that's something noble and tragic, but it's not noble and tragic, it's pathetic.'

'And you?' said Xeno. 'Are you all at once the expert on love?'

'He doesn't need to be an expert,' said Perdita. 'He just needs to try.' She went to Zel and held his hand. Xeno nodded, smiling a smile that was not a smile.

"Love is the unfamiliar name behind the hands that wove the intolerable shirt of flame."

★ ★ ★

He pulled his T-shirt over his head. There were scars across his shoulders. He unbuckled his belt, undid the buttons of his flies and stepped out of his jeans. He turned his back to them both and took off his boxers.

His hips held the faded red lines of the operation to rebuild his pelvis. But that wasn't it; it was the tattoo.

Sweeping up from his sacroiliac joints on either side of his torso and meeting at his fifth thoracic vertebra was a pair of wings.

'I thought I could fly,' said Xeno, 'but I could only fall.'

Interval

Zel drove Perdita home.

Through the wide streets and hard lights and big cars. Lives that never stop.

Lives that never start. Workers walking, drunks falling, cabs slowing and speeding away. A dog at the trash, a woman at the window, a black man asleep on a folded billboard in the doorway of a discount store.

EVERYTHING MUST GO

The hotel with its hookers hanging round the lobby. The nightman giving them coffee. The 24/7 laundromat steamy and bright-lit. A child awake too late, his mother holding his hand. He falls every third step and she rights him, a nylon luggage bag over her shoulder. Broken zipper. She's talking to him all the time but she's looking straight ahead.

A boy telling his girl how it is. She's on her phone.

A nun waiting for the night-bus. Bus comes. Nun gone.

And you and me in the car where we've always been, where we'll always be, this night, this road, even when we're gone and the road is gone and the city is gone but we'll be here because everything is imprinted forever with what it once was.

The house and bar were in darkness. It was nearly 3am.

Zel killed the engine and let the car roll down the track till it came to a halt under its own weight. He pulled the brake on its ratchet.

Perdita climbed out so that Clo wouldn't hear the car door.

'Zel?'

And the stairs were dark and he held her hand and she took him up to her room and she didn't put on the light. They undressed quickly because they were shy. Perdita got into bed. Zel lay next to her, the blood in his body like a private Niagara. She put her arms round him.

'I'm glad you're not my brother.'

★ ★ ★

In this night-soaked bed with you it is courage for the day I seek. That when the light comes I will turn towards it. Nothing could be simpler. Nothing could be harder. And in the morning we will get dressed together and go.

In the game, Xeno had defeated an Angel and taken his wings. For a short time he could fly. Not for long. Part of the game was to avoid falling when the wings failed — as they always did — like Icarus staring at the sun.

But now he could move upwards through the feathery snow and snowy feathers and look in through MiMi's window. He held himself there in slow swoops, looking in.

She was as she was. Lying like a tomb knight in a chapel. White and made of stone. The room with the double windows that overlooked Notre Dame was a tiny white world where nothing moved or changed. She was Sleeping Beauty who wouldn't wake up. There was no kiss.

She was always here but she could be elsewhere. Walking like a statue through a statue garden. Alive and not alive. Sleeping and not sleeping. She is by the river sometimes. They say it's her.

Xeno fluttered at the window like a moth.

He wasn't her only visitor. Leo came and hurled himself at the glass that would not break. Battered the building with his wings. Promised. Begged. Raged. Wept. On the windowsill on his knees in a snowstorm of his own making.

Nothing changed.

THREE

Ghosts That Walk

Pauline had arranged for Sicilia to meet local residents at the Roundhouse in London's Chalk Farm, to discuss Sicilia's plans to demolish the theatre and rebuild the site with two twenty-storey towers for what the architects called 'purposeful contemporary living'.

Included in the plan was a purposeful purpose-built 250-seat theatre with funding guaranteed for ten years. And there was a block of purposefully affordable homes facing the mainline railway into Euston Station.

The purposefully affordable homes were purposefully low-rise, screened from the prestige part of the development behind a wall of water designed by the artist Roni Horn. The wall of water's purposeful purpose was to protect the luxury apartments from railway noise.

Critics said that life in the affordable homes would be like life behind a perpetually flushing toilet.

'Give people something for nothing and they complain,' said Leo. 'When they pay for it they appreciate it.'

'Not everybody likes water,' said Pauline. 'Especially designed water designed to keep them out.'

'What about the Living Forest? OK, so it's a DESIGNED living forest (bitch). This is a development surrounded by birch trees

— romantic as Old Russia.'

'That will make your purchasers feel at home,' said Pauline.

'You're always negative,' said Leo. 'Why hooray when you can oy vey?'

'You are a purpose-built shmuck,' said Pauline. 'The houses on the railway line won't see the living forest any more than they will see the waterfall. You should give them something green.'

'So throw in a year's supply of tinned peas.'

'Leo! If you want this to go smoothly be realistic!'

'It will go smoothly! I've bribed everybody. By which I mean I've given everybody who matters something of what they want. I've funded the arts, paid for a local crèche, designated land for low-paid key workers in London and . . . '

'So give the housing association a playground for the kids. That's what they want.'

'Kids don't go out unless you force them to go out. Kids have no idea that OUTSIDE even exists. They do school, car, bedroom, friends' bedrooms, more car, shopping, Facebook, Twitter, eBay, online porn, beach. They only know there is a sun because they have to wear sunscreen to protect their pale little faces.'

'Have you lost touch with everything about the real world?'

'What? Poverty is real and money isn't?'

'Something along those lines — in fact, for you, that's profound.'

Leo looked pleased. 'Can I use it in one of my charity talks?'

Pauline raised her eyes to where she would be going if the Jews believed in an afterlife. 'The kids in the affordable houses need a playground.'

'What, so they can smoke skunk and have a freezing shag on a broken swing?'

'Sixty per cent of the children in the Affordable Living will be under ten.'

'That's who I was talking about! The playground idea is just a fantasy of childhood.'

'But Old Russia birch trees and Zen water is uber-reality?'

'I am not only selling to the Russians and the Chinese!'

'That's true — you're selling to anyone with a million or so to get started.'

'Since when were you poor?'

'Since when did money have no conscience?'

Leo had wanted to kill Pauline since the day he met her — but more than thirty years later she was still alive and kicking (him). How had he allowed this to happen?

'So where would we put this fantasy playground? I know!' Leo clapped his hands and punched the air-conditioned air. 'Let's put it in Israel! How come you never relocated to Israel? Live the dream, sister.'

Leo took a pencil and drew angry arrows all over his plans like a convicted serial killer flagging the bodies.

'I'm not moving the yoga studio or the sushi bar or the quad bike and ski shed or the guest suites or the outdoor heated swimming pool or the on-site porter's bungalow.'

'It's not a bungalow — it's a garage with a

shower behind the fridge.'

'It's a fantastic perk — a job with living quarters.'

'Quarter is right — it's a quarter of the size of the penthouse dog kennel.'

'Vladimir Oshitavitch has four dogs and he's bought the penthouse off-plan for an undisclosed sum.'

'So he needs to bring his huskies to pull his sledge to Harrods?'

'Can't you read a drawing? The site is full. Spacious and gracious. And FULL.'

'So take a slice out of the car-parking.'

'The apartments need two car spaces each. If I dig any deeper I might as well start fracking.'

'You mean you didn't buy the energy rights?'

'Oh, fuck off.'

'Will you listen to me?'

'Like I have any choice?'

'Sell eight of the apartments as zero-carbon. The smallest ones. Pied-à-terre becomes eco-terre. Make it sound like it's doing good in the world. And you know what? It IS doing good in the world. You know that old saying?'

'Spare me,' said Leo.

'The more you give the more you get.'

Pauline took a thick marker-pen from the pen-pot on the desk and wrote on the vast plan pinned on the wall the word 'PLAY'.

Leo snatched the pen off her. Pauline held on. Leo pulled and won.

'FUCK, FUCK, FUCK! Now I've got PEN all over my SHIRT! Just tell me this, Pauline of the forty fucking years in the wilderness: HOW MUCH good do I have to do in the world?'

Pauline said, 'Is that a real question?'

Leo didn't hold her gaze. There was another time, before it happened, and it was like a place he could see and never go back to, because you can't go back in time, can you? It's not a real question.

'This has to stop some time, Pauline.'

'I didn't start it. I can't stop it.'

Leo wrote GROUND next to PLAY.

* ⋆ ⋆

It was evening and Leo was walking home. His office was in Shepherd's Market, long since lost of its sheep. He liked to walk home to his house in Westminster, not far from the Thames.

After it had happened, and he and MiMi were divorcing, he had sold their house in Little Venice and moved the offices. To stay was like hitting himself in the face with his fist.

He walked along the river every night. He didn't know why. Why do we do the things we do?

And that night he was thinking about MiMi.

⋆ ⋆ ⋆

He didn't think about MiMi because he couldn't think about her. She was radioactive. She had to be sealed.

The memory of her had to be encased in waterproof concrete. He didn't deny what he

253

had done or the consequences of what he had done. To think about that was to think about himself. His stupidity. His jealousy. His crime. He knew how to think about himself.

But her? It was the thought of her that threatened him. He could not allow her inside his head.

That she had become a recluse made it easier. After the newspapers and the TV programme and the accusations and the contempt and the celebrity discussions and the in-depth superficiality and the exclusive content, it happened as it always does and everyone forgot.

There were sightings of her, in dark glasses and a scruffy coat.

Is that her, early morning, getting coffee in a paper cup before they've finished washing the floor of the café, and the chairs are still up on the tables?

Is that her, going down the steps by Notre Dame to the Seine, before 7am, and there's no one around except a square-shaped woman with a long-shaped dog? The woman notices her most mornings, walking with her head down as far as the mouth of the Canal Saint-Martin, where she stands like a statue, her hands in her pockets, watching the water that has no memory and wanting to be like water.

She does this every day.

They say it's her.

And the cars begin on the roads above as regular as time, one day the same as any other but for sun or rain. And do we reach enlightenment by setting out or by sitting still?

And what is enlightenment anyway but delusions we can live with?

She wonders about that.

Paris is full of angels. Every day she finds another carving, another statue and she imagines what it would be like if they came to life. And who trapped them in stone? She feels trapped in stone.

She remembers what Michelangelo said; that when he took a block of granite or marble he saw the figure trapped there and his duty was to free it.

See him, sweat-soaked and dust-coated, chiselling free a toe, a finger, a tight belt of stomach muscle, the upward pull of a tricep, the clean line of the clavicle. The closed life made visible.

But what sculptor out of hell had taken a living woman and rendered her flesh and carved her into a monument of herself?

She was held in time as they all were, the statues, friezes, reliefs, that watched and watched over the changing city. She was one of them.

The present that disappears like water over the waterfall. The rush of time that passes so slowly and so fast. How long has it been?

She walks to stop herself standing still. As though she could walk out of time, put it behind her where it belongs. But she can't because it's always there, right in front of her, the past is right in front of her and every day she walks slam into it like a door that locks the future on the other side.

She keeps walking but nothing is moving and

nothing is changing. And at the end of her morning walk when she stands still for a long time she feels that this, at least, has some reality to it.

Maybe it's someone else. Maybe it's not her. There's no shortage of heartbreak.

★ ★ ★

Leo arrived home. The lights were on because he had programmed the timer. Why can't you have time on a timer?

Switch it on when you want it? Switch it off when you don't? Switch off time at night — why waste it while you sleep? Switch off, Leo. Just switch off.

He got a drink. Vodka. Ice.

He went upstairs. There was a room where he kept her clothes. She had never come back to their house before he had sold it. She had never taken anything away. Like a dead person she had gone forever, leaving everything behind. So he had kept her clothes. And when he moved into this house he had a room made that was her dressing room, except that she never got dressed in it. Or undressed in it.

Her body. Don't think about her body.

★ ★ ★

The clothes were just as she had left them. Racks of her but not her. Plastic dress-protectors, suit-carriers, coat hangers, bags. Dresses on one side, skirts and shirts on the other side. Cedar shelves of sweaters and T-shirts. Leo stood like a man who has broken into a room where he doesn't belong.

He picked up a sweater from the shelves and unfolded it. He buried his face in it. He sat down, his back against the wall, knees up, his head resting on his arms.

No excuses. No reasons. No forgiveness. No hope.

I Would Not Prize Them
Without Her Love

Perdita and Zel had come to London.

She'd slept with her head against his shoulder through the noisy night of other people's packed-together lives.

For the last few hours they had been waiting to check into their room at the King's Cross Travelodge.

'How much money do we have?'

'Enough for three weeks.'

★ ★ ★

Perdita had taken the $1000 in the attaché case — she reckoned it was hers — and Zel had paid for the flights.

Perdita had left a long voicemail for Clo. Zel had just disappeared.

At last the tired woman in the tight suit gave them the keys to their room. It wasn't big and it wasn't beautiful but it was theirs. Zel began putting his T-shirts in a drawer. Perdita was running a shower. He stood and watched her. He loved the miracle of her body. How could she be so beautiful? He unfolded the towel for her and wrapped her in it, holding her to him. 'What's the plan?'

'I'll go to his office tomorrow.'

'I'll come with you.'

'I have to do this part by myself.'

'But he knows me.'

'He knew you when you were eight!'

Perdita went into the bedroom. Zel followed her.

'I don't want you to go on your own.'

She shrugged like she was dismissing him. He took her wrists. Too tight.

'Let go of me! I'm not your possession.'

Zel let go. 'I'm sorry.' He sat on the bed, his body absolutely still the way it was when he was upset. Like a hiding animal. 'I guess I'm taking it out on you.'

'What?'

'That you'll suddenly find a whole new family and forget about me.'

Perdita sat next to him on the bed. She took his hand. 'I'm not going to forget you.'

★   ★   ★

Sicilia Ltd was above an art gallery. Two young men in tailored suits were directing a smart black van to unload. They smiled at Perdita because she was pretty. 'Are you looking for a job? Come and work for us.'

Perdita shook her head and buzzed the intercom. There was no answer. One of the young men took out a bunch of keys and opened the door. 'Don't tell her.'

'Who?'

'You'll see. Would you like to go out for a drink tonight?'

He was handsome, confident, floppy hair. Perdita smiled and shook her head. He sighed.

'If you change your mind — I'm Adam.'

He stood back to let Perdita up the wide, well-carpeted stairs to the first floor. Tracey Emin prints lined the walls.

The Receptionist had only just gone upstairs herself and she came out of the ladies' as Perdita appeared in the big, comfortable, quietly expensive waiting area, its walls hung with drawings this time, not prints. There was a big neon sign that said RISK-VALUE.

'Who let you in?' said the Receptionist.

'I'm here to enquire about an internship,' said Perdita.

The Receptionist was six feet tall and perfectly made-up. Her legs were long, sleek and threatening. Perdita was wearing a simple summer dress, strappy sandals and no make-up. She wasn't tall. The Receptionist looked at her without smiling.

'Did you send in your CV?'

'Yes.'

'Mrs Levy isn't here today.'

'What about Mr Kaiser?'

'Mr Kaiser has appointments all day.'

'I'll wait here,' said Perdita, sitting down with such finality on one of the linen-covered sofas that the Receptionist could do nothing but swing her computer screen round to block Perdita from her view.

There was a name block on her desk. Lorraine LaTrobe.

'Are you from New Orleans? I wondered because LaTrobe is a Louisiana name. I'm from New Bohemia.'

'I'm not,' said Miss LaTrobe, swivelling her chair to mark an end to the exchange.

Perdita waited.

After about an hour Leo arrived. He was heavier than she had expected. He had less hair than she had imagined. Xeno's photograph was not this man but this was the man.

Leo glanced at her. 'Morning, Lorraine. Pauline here yet?'

'Good morning, Mr Kaiser. Mrs Levy isn't in today.'

'Why not? She finally dropped dead?'

'She's booked out in the Diary today and tomorrow.'

'Did you tell me?'

'It's in the Diary,' said Miss LaTrobe again, as though the Diary was a confident scripture to turn to in times of need.

'If I wanted to look at the Diary myself I could save money on a PA,' said Leo. 'Where's my PA? Or is Virginia booked out as well?'

'Yes, she is.'

Leo turned to Perdita. 'Who are you?'

'She's waiting to see Mrs Levy. I told her Mrs Levy isn't in the Diary today.'

Leo looked at Perdita again. 'Are you from the housing association? About the Roundhouse project?'

Perdita shook her head. She couldn't speak.

Leo said, 'I thought I recognised you.'

'She wants an internship,' said Miss LaTrobe, making it sound like a colonic torpedo suppository.

Leo grimaced and went to the lift. The doors

closed across his back but Perdita saw him for a second in the mirror, still frowning at her.

'When is Mrs Levy back?' said Perdita.

'According to the Diary, Monday,' said Miss LaTrobe, without moving her lips or making eye contact.

Perdita thought she would be a great ventriloquist. But she continued to sit on the sofa. And Miss LaTrobe continued to ignore her.

At five minutes to 1pm Leo reappeared to go to lunch.

'Excuse me . . . ' said Perdita.

'You need to see Pauline,' said Leo.

'I told her that,' said Miss LaTrobe.

★ ★ ★

At 2.30pm Leo returned. Perdita stood up and pushed back her heavy hair. Leo smiled at her before he realised he was smiling. Something in the way she . . .

'Come back tomorrow,' he said. 'Pauline will be here.'

'Not according to the Diary,' said Miss LaTrobe, standing up to her full height, which was several inches above Leo.

'Oh, pardon me for having an opinion,' said Leo. Then he said, 'Did Pauline hire you?'

'Yes,' said Miss LaTrobe. 'Personally.'

'I am outnumbered and outmanoeuvred,' said Leo. He looked at Perdita. 'Did you have an appointment today?'

'I've been in the States longer than expected,' said Perdita, 'or I would have been here before.'

265

'I'll be down at 7pm,' said Leo. 'Your call.'
And then he went back up to his office.

★ ★ ★

'Don't get your hopes up,' said Miss LaTrobe.

'Why not?' said Perdita.

The Receptionist shrugged. Another day. Another idiot.

What am I doing here? thought Perdita. *If I leave now it's over. I've seen him. He didn't want me. Why do I want him?*

★ ★ ★

At 6pm Miss LaTrobe announced her departure. Like she was a flight to Miami. 'I'm afraid you will have to leave, as you can't stay here unsupervised.'

'I won't steal anything,' said Perdita.

'It's the Rules,' said Miss LaTrobe. Clearly the Rules offered as much certainty as the Diary, so Perdita suggested she call Mr Kaiser.

'I can't interrupt him.'

'Tell him I won't leave,' said Perdita.

The Receptionist rolled her eyes, pulled a face, tapped her (impressive) fingernails on the desk and spoke to Leo. 'Thank you, Mr Kaiser. And yes, certainly I shall let Miss Tchaikovsky know that you cannot meet her for dinner tonight as you are working late.'

★ ★ ★

Miss LaTrobe disappeared into the ladies' and reappeared ten minutes later in an orange one-piece Lycra cycling suit. 'You are to wait here,' she said to Perdita.

'Do you cycle home?' said Perdita, because it was something to say.

'No. I work in a fetish club,' said Miss LaTrobe and, taking her orange helmet from the desk drawer, she left the building.

★ ★ ★

Around 7pm Leo came back down in the lift. He had taken off his tie. He needed to shave.

'So you waited?'

She nodded.

'What's your name?'

'Miranda.'

'Miranda who?'

'Shepherd.'

'OK, Miranda Shepherd — so come and have a drink and tell me all about yourself. Patience is its own reward, or some shit I never believed in. Where did patience ever get you except to the back of the queue? But in your case . . . '

★ ★ ★

The evening was warm. Pink sky. Red buses. Black cabs. Lights coming on across the city. The evening feel of home-time. A man giving out free newspapers. STANDARD! STANDARD! Young men crowding the pavements outside the pubs. Tired faces, shirtsleeves, women in heels that hurt. The queue at the check-out for something to eat in front of the TV. The crowds flowing down into the underground.

'There's a bar by the river,' said Leo. 'We can have langoustines and vodka. It's Thursday.'

'Does that make a difference?' said Perdita.

'I like a routine. These days.'

★ ★ ★

The bar was busy and noisy but the barman raised his hand to Leo and, without anything being said, there was a table just inside/outside in the long window that opened onto a narrow terrace, and a bottle of Grey Goose from the freezer in an ice bucket, and a set of tins of tonic water and fresh sliced lemons and limes.

'They know me,' said Leo.

'Can I have a mineral water with the lime?' said Perdita.

★ ★ ★

Perdita was talking but Leo wasn't listening. He was nodding and meeting her eyes but he wasn't listening. She must be twenty-one or twenty-two. What was wrong with that? Youth is so irresistible. Irreplaceable. And wasted on the young.

'Responsible capitalism,' said Leo, surprising himself that he had heard her question. 'That's Sicilia.'

'What does your wife do?' said Perdita.

'I'm divorced,' said Leo. 'What about you?'

'I'm not divorced,' said Perdita. 'Do you have children?'

He looked down. 'No. No, I don't have children.'

She nearly said . . . Instead she took another langoustine. She didn't know how expensive they were. At home they weren't expensive at all.

She was eating more than him. The women he took out didn't eat. They ordered food but they didn't eat it. She was unselfconscious. She wasn't trying to please him. Leo liked her. She asked him why he wasn't eating, and he didn't say *My heart is full of something that takes my mind from feasting.*

He ripped into a langoustine.

'I come here because I like the river,' he said. 'I like it that the Thames is older than London — that mammoths drank here once.'

'It's so narrow,' said Perdita. 'The Mississippi is like a world. Did you ever see it?'

'Yes,' said Leo. 'I had a friend who lived in New Bohemia. It was a long time ago. That's what happens as you get older; everything is a long time ago.'

'But not the present,' said Perdita. 'That's now.'

'You're young. You have a present because you don't have a past. When I was young I lived in Paris for a year. I was working there. I fell in love with the river — the Seine; actually I fell in love with someone. Perhaps that's why I find water mysterious and romantic. I'm not just talking about boy meets girl, I mean something bigger — about longing, I suppose. The Germans call it *verlangen*. My father was German.'

'Was she French? The woman you fell in love with?'

'Yes. Petite, boyish, but feminine. Like you.'

Perdita blushed. Leo misunderstood. 'It's just a compliment. Take it.'

'Thank you,' said Perdita.

They looked out at the water. The strings of lights. The boats that came in close to the pier.

Leo felt at ease and excited. What's happening to me? he thought, and This is ridiculous.

He tried to focus. 'Miranda, we're organising a big charity concert — it happens next weekend; maybe you would like to be part of that? To see how you do with us? It's mostly music. A few acts.'

'I sing in a girl-group at home,' said Perdita. 'We're called The Separations.'

'That is a great name! What do you sing?'

'Retro-classics. My dad is a fantastic pianist. I've been singing since I was born.'

'Have you?' His eyes were dark with the unsaid.

'Yes. Are you OK? Is there . . . ?'

He interrupted her. 'It's nothing. But these nothings . . . they . . . '

* * *

These nothings are nothing. But the sky is nothing, the earth is nothing, I am nothing, love is nothing, loss is nothing.

* * *

The evening was cooling into night. Perdita thanked Leo.

'We can go on somewhere if you want — show you London.'

She shook her head. He offered her a cab. 'I can walk,' she said, 'I like walking. I can follow the map on my phone. It isn't far.'

But it is, he thought, watching her walk away. It might as well be the moon, the distance that separated him from a life that is good.

★   ★   ★

Leo got out of the cab at his house. His lights were on. He unlocked the door and switched them off. There was nothing to see. His games console was lit up like an aquarium.

Xeno had brought in a new player. They had been collecting feathers. Sweet. As though the world could be saved by hard work and hope. Leo opened his six wings and flew low over the city looking for feathers to set on fire. Looking for feathers to douse into Sunken Angels.

He flew up to the top of the Sorbonne. '*Sicut umbra dies nostri*,' says the Sundial Angel: *Our days flee like a shadow.*

He prefers her sister. She's ready for him — the one bared to the waist with the hard, high, round breasts. Part boy, part girl. Legs open with a book she's never read. He's erect.

One pair of wings kept him upright while he was on her. The second pair held her hard gold body against him. The third pair he pushed out behind him, an upward flag like the retractable fin on his car. It was a fuck you. To traffic. To Xeno. To himself. Fuck you, Leo. Fuck you.

He falls back, done.

★　★　★

Leo woke up on the sofa. He put on the light. 3am. The small hours when life curls in on itself like a world not ready to open. The radio had turned itself on.

There was a woman talking: '*A thousand knees ten thousand years together, naked, fasting, upon a barren mountain, and still winter in storm perpetual, could not move the gods to look the way thou wert.*'

★　★　★

Leo sat up, groggy, sweaty, scratchy, dry-mouthed. He went upstairs, falling over his undone trousers. He stepped out of them, and in his socks and jockeys, his shirt and noosed tie, got in the shower, stripping off as the water fell over him.

He left his clothes in a sodden heap on the shower floor. He shaved, dressed, made coffee and drank it down in one searing swig.

He got in his car. No radio. No thoughts. Only the backward pull of time.

That day . . .

★　★　★

Leo was in the queue at Passport Control. The man checking documents asked him to stand aside a moment. The next thing he knew, three policemen were checking his details and asking what he'd done with the baby.

Then it happened.

Leo arguing with the police. The police arguing with Leo. All big guys. All at the same height. The little Indian passport-checker was trying to pretend that nothing was happening as he processed other people coming through, all staring at Leo.

The police were confused because Leo had no baby. Leo said his wife had post-natal depression. He was taking their son on holiday to give her a break. The police looked at Milo's passport — is this your father? Yes.

The big guys went back to arguing — no one cared about Milo.

There was a man lived in an airport.

Milo moved steadily, quietly backwards, away from them, their backs to him in an angry circle. No one would notice.

Milo was round the corner and going towards the security lanes. There was a family over in Lane Four. He ran over to them — if anyone saw him they thought he was just catching up. He put his backpack on the metal conveyor belt. He walked through the metal detector. He looked round. He was in the airport. Maybe he could find Tony.

★ ★ ★

Milo had tagged on to a family and gone through Security. He couldn't see Tony. There were a lot of people. He heard his name announced over the Tannoy. He was to go to Information.

Milo couldn't find Information for a while, then when he saw it his father wasn't there — only the two policemen were there. He turned back the other way.

Soon Milo was in the skytrain, which sounded exciting but wasn't. Then he was at B Gate and C Gate and then back to B Gate. Then he joined a queue for a plane and he was small and seemed to belong and only when he was through Boarding and halfway down the stairs did the woman realise he wasn't with the others and they didn't have his passport and boarding card. She called him back. He ran. She was the police. He didn't run onto the plane, he ran down the second flight of stairs and through the wide-open door where they were taking some luggage on a flat trolley. HEY! HEY! But Milo was running, round the corner of the building and into the path of a repair truck.

Superman, rewind time.

★ ★ ★

Leo parked his car near the gates of Highgate Cemetery. If there was a burial that morning someone would be there. He knew the routine. If they were there they would let him in.

He walked down the paths guarded by mourning angels. Milo was buried near the west

274

wall. Leo had bought the plot at a charity auction before Milo was born. He had bid a fortune to get it. The cemetery was long since full and it was world-famous. The right challenge for Leo. He could have bought a studio flat for what he paid. And now Milo was in it. The bones of him by now, Leo thought. Nothing to know of him except the past.

Leo stood for a long time as the sun came up bright and clear. The past was always in front of him like a river he couldn't cross.

He went and filled the water container and picked two of the wild roses growing in the hedge. 'MiMi and Milo,' he said as he put the thorny stems into the water. He got up and turned to go. The gardener was near by, working quietly with a hoe. Checked shirt, sleeves rolled up past the elbows. 'Hi Tony!' called Leo.

The gardener turned. 'I'm Pete.'

Leo raised a hand. Of course it wasn't Tony. Tony is dead.

⋆   ⋆   ⋆

Perdita and Zel were lying on the bed in the Travelodge, watching TV with the sound turned down.

'So what's he like?' said Zel.

'All I could think about was that this man gave me away.'

'To my dad! Are you going to tell him it's you?'

'I don't know. If I do, he'll be in my life. And he's pretty controlling.'

'I looked it up,' said Zel. 'It doesn't usually work out.'

'What doesn't?'

'Adoption reunions. Everybody wants something they can never have. Life can't unhappen.'

'I don't want Life to unhappen. Then I wouldn't have Shep or Clo or HollyPollyMolly.'

'But you would have me,' said Zel. 'How weird is that?'

Perdita rolled herself into him. 'You mean it's fate?'

'I don't know. We used to discuss this all the time when I was studying philosophy. Is life just a series of accidents that from a distance look like patterns? Like when you see fields and rivers and houses from a plane window and they look beautiful and sane, whereas on the ground they're just what they are — random or even ugly.'

'Dad says things are meant to be.'

'Have you spoken to him?'

'He'll be mad at me. I should have told him we were leaving.'

'You couldn't.'

'No. I couldn't. Do you think we'll end up like Leo and Xeno?'

'Complete assholes?'

'Sad people.'

'They weren't always sad.'

'That's worse. They had a life and they destroyed it. Their own and other people's.'

'We'll do it better,' said Zel. 'We'll go back home, we'll make a life, and we'll show our own kids how to be brave and true.'

276

'We just met!'

'Am I going too fast?'

She kissed him. 'Yes. Much too fast.'

'I thought girls want boys who can commit?'

She hit him with a pillow. She felt a pulse of relaxation. She realised how tense she had been all day.

'Zel . . . thanks for coming with me. I'm a lot to take on right now. I know that . . . '

He put his arm round her. 'We're here. We're doing it. Let's do it. Do you want to look for your mother too?'

'I don't know. This is harder than I thought.'

'How so?'

'Upsetting. I thought I wouldn't feel anything — I mean, I don't know Leo. I just met him today.'

Zel held her close. 'But you have met your mother. You lived inside her.'

And that was true and Perdita felt it to be true and that was the part that was hardest. How can you be connected to someone with whom you have no connection?

'Do you look like Leo?' said Zel.

'I don't think so. He's old and bald and a bit fat! Same mouth maybe. I look like my mother — that is, how she used to look. But we don't know what she looks like now. There are no recent images — just someone who might be her in dark glasses and a hat.'

'It probably is her — only celebrities think dark glasses and a hat is how you blend into the crowd.'

'She's not famous now.'

'Is it weird for you that she was?'

'It's all weird. That's just one weirdness in the weird.'

Zel flipped off the TV. 'Do you think you can sleep?'

'No.'

'Then let's go out.'

'It's midnight!'

'So? This is London. Come on.'

⋆ ⋆ ⋆

They go out. They're just kids. They find a night-bus. Then walk through to Soho. Italian ice cream. His arm round her shoulders. Her arm round his waist. They walk through Chinatown and Covent Garden and across the Aldwych down to Waterloo Bridge and stand in the middle looking west and east, and there's Big Ben telling clock time, and down below there's the Thames flowing liquid time, and in the small space they occupy their own time is real. Not the past, not the future, this now.

He doesn't take a photo or a video because he wants to remember — by which he means he wants to misremember because the moment is made up of what the camera can't capture.

And the river takes the night away and they go back to bed and sleep and the city dreams itself into another day.

⋆ ⋆ ⋆

In the morning, early, Perdita's phone rings. It's Leo.

'Hi, Miranda. Leo here. Meet me at the Roundhouse in an hour.'

'Where?' says Perdita. What's he talking about?

Leo wants to be impatient but isn't because he wants to see her. He softens his voice. 'Northern Line. The black one. Chalk Farm. Or Camden Town and then you walk. OK? About 11am.'

★ ★ ★

This time Zel comes with her. They get out of the underground at Chalk Farm. There are a lot of people waving banners that say SAVE OUR BUILDING.

Perdita and Zel make their way into the crowd. There's a guy with a megaphone. Police on horseback. Perdita asks a young woman with a placard what's going on.

'Fuckin' rich buying the whole fuckin' place.'

Then she sees Leo shouting angrily into his phone. She said to Zel, 'There he is.'

'Is that him? Is that Leo?'

'You don't recognise him?'

'Not without his hair. And he wasn't fat.'

'He's seen me. You should go — I'll text.'

Perdita ran across the road. She's lovely, thought Leo, watching her, and she has no idea that she is. His current date was a Russian lingerie model who Vaped during sex.

Leo was smiling. 'Good you could come, Miranda. I thought if you're going to intern with us you should see our next project. It's quite a building, isn't it?'

Just then the crowd started chanting — 'OUT OUT OUT. OUT OUT OUT.'

'We'd better get inside,' said Leo. 'Security can handle this.'

Leo put his hand on the small of Perdita's back and bundled her through the doors.

'Good morning, Mr Kaiser,' said the security man. Leo relaxed. He was back in his world.

'Let me show you round, Miranda. This place was built as a turning shed for the trams. Trams can't reverse, so this is where they changed direction — by going round in a circle — in this vast theatre space here. Pretty impressive, isn't it?'

Perdita was looking at the framed posters on the bare brick walls. Circus, theatre, bands, and then she saw it — MiMi at the Roundhouse. She wasn't listening to Leo. He didn't notice.

'Underneath — directly below us — is where the machinery was kept: the cogs, chains, engines that turned the plates. For a long time it's been an entertainment venue — now it's time for a new life. Come up to the gallery.'

He put his hand on her shoulder and escorted her up the stairs. Outside she could hear police sirens.

'Why are you pulling it down?'

'The site is fantastic and there's no public money any more for places like this. You can't subsidise everything forever — nice as that would be. Private money has to fill the gap. I'm building a small theatre space and some public

280

housing — because I like to think I am socially aware. The centrepiece will be a pair of incredible apartment towers — some of the most beautiful lateral living in London.'

'What is everyone protesting about, then?'

'People don't like change, Miranda. It's human nature. And money has a bad press these days. None of those people outside pay tax — well, not much tax — but they hate people like me who really are the people supporting the country. What I am doing is saving this place — they can't see that. But you've got an economics degree — did you say Harvard?'

'No,' said Perdita.

'Yes, I thought you said Harvard. You'll find out for yourself as you make money just how easy it is to be misunderstood. All I am trying to do is help everyone and they treat me like a tyrant.'

Leo and Perdita arrived in the gallery. Leo leaned on the rail and looked down. 'You see the stage? We'll do a final concert. It's part of the deal — a fully funded farewell week culminating in a musicfest for Save the Children. Then the wrecking ball arrives.'

'Why are you knocking it down?'

'We're reusing all the Victorian bricks.'

'Why are you knocking it down?'

'We have planning permission.'

'Why are you knocking it down?'

'Is this a knock-knock joke? Do Americans do knock-knock jokes? Were you born in New Bohemia?'

'MiMi sang here, didn't she?'

Leo looked straight ahead over the gallery rail. 'She was my wife in those days,' he said.

Leo turned and went towards the stairs. 'I just wanted you to see the building.'

★ ★ ★

At the foot of the stairs a security man in a suit with a walkie-talkie came over to Leo. 'Someone called Ronnie is waiting for you.'

'Ronnie?'

'Says he's the artist. From New York. Out there.'

Leo looked through the glass at the demon-strators on the street. A short-cropped figure was standing at the front with a placard that said ARTISTS AGAINST ASSHOLES.

'That's Roni Horn and she's a woman.' Leo walked swiftly out of the door, holding out his hand and smiling. 'Roni! Roni! It's an honour!'

Roni Horn didn't look like she was an honour. She looked dangerous. She said, 'You told me my wall of water was for the community. You have turned it into water-boarding against the poor. Who wants to sleep next to a wall of water?'

'We can adjust the plans,' said Leo, 'don't worry! This is an honour. Can I get a photograph with you? Jerry! Jerry!' Leo waved his smart-phone at the man from Security and moved in closer to Roni. He went to put his arm around her. She pushed him away.

'I am here to protest!'

The crowd cheered and the chanting began again: OUT OUT OUT OUT OUT. Leo's mood changed like a weather-storm. 'Didn't I buy that wall of water from you? Did I misunderstand something? Weren't you paid?'

'I was paid. I wasn't bought,' said Roni.

'If I buy a painting from you and you don't like where I hang it — too bad. If I buy a wall of water from you and you don't like where I put it — too bad! You know why artists can afford to shout about their values? Because people like me are paying your bills.'

Perdita was behind Leo. She said, 'Don't talk to her like that!'

Leo rounded on Perdita. 'Who do you think you are?'

Perdita looked at Leo. She said nothing. Perdita looked at Leo and he flinched like she had slapped him. He thought . . . he almost thought . . . but he was thinking of MiMi. Somebody threw a brick. Was that a brick? The past hit him in the face like a brick.

He tried to speak but his face hurt. Then there was a surge from the crowd pushing forward as the police dragged a tarpaulin from under a group of protestors sitting down in front of the building.

Perdita saw Zel jostling to get through the press. He was arguing with a security guard. The guard shoved him. Zel shoved back. 'Zel!' shouted Perdita. 'ZEL!'

Leo turned in slow motion. *What did she say?* What was happening to time? He felt like time was being demolished brick by brick. The walled place was falling.

Leo saw Zel. Zel? *No, it couldn't be him. It wasn't Tony in the cemetery this morning.* He wiped his face with the back of his hand. Blood from where the brick had hit him. Everyone was shouting. He couldn't hear.

Perdita thought — *Leo looks like he's seen a ghost* — and wondered what anybody means by that because nobody does see ghosts — but still we look like we've seen them . . .

Zel darted forward. The security man stepped between him and Leo. Leo shook his head. The security man took a step back.

'Zel . . . ? Xeno's Zel?'

'Yes,' said Zel.

'What are you doing here?'

'He's with me,' said Perdita.

'You know each other?'

'She's my girlfriend.'

'Will you shut up?' said Perdita.

'Miranda is your girlfriend?'

'No . . . P — '

'SHUT UP!' shouted Perdita. Leo looked surprised. He was the one who did the shouting.

'Is Xeno here?'

Here in Your City

Shep had recovered well.

There was no damage, physical or mental. Perdita had known that when she boarded the plane but still she didn't want to tell Shep what she was doing. She saw him in the afternoon and went straight to the airport to meet Zel for the short flight to Dallas and then the night flight to London.

Clo got her voicemail but he didn't tell Shep either. What was he going to say? But the day after Shep wanted to know why Perdita hadn't come to see him.

Clo was silent.

Shep sat up in bed, looking at his son. 'You told her about the BabyHatch, didn't you?'

Clo was silent. Shep nodded and he didn't speak for a while. Then he said, 'Now it's started we'd better finish it. You listen to me.'

★　★　★

That afternoon Clo drove round to Autolycus and got the address he needed. 'Am I missing something?' said Autolycus. 'Because I don't like to miss anything.'

'Ask Dad,' said Clo.

I might just damn well do that, thought Autolycus as Clo drove away.

Clo was soon outside the deserted house. He

buzzed the entry phone. No answer. So he backed his Chevy across the heavy gates, climbed on the roof and jumped down into the driveway. He hammered on the door and shouted and hammered some more. Then he wrapped his fist in his jacket and smashed the big, gracious window that Perdita had left unshuttered and unbarred. He was in.

'Spooky fright-night,' said Clo, looking at the empty fireplace and musty armchairs. He went into the hall. He could hear music from upstairs. Rickie Lee Jones. Good choice. He ran up the stairs two at a time.

Clo opened the attic door. Xeno was staring at some giant screen covered in feathers.

'Beano — get it together. Shep wants to talk to you.'

★ ★ ★

Outside the Roundhouse Leo was trying to hear Lorraine LaTrobe. She was standing in the offices of Sicilia, arms folded across her leather Chanel suit, talking into her speakerphone.

'Three men. Two black. One gay.'

'Get Pauline!'

'She is on her way.'

Leo pushed through the protesters to the road. He was jostled, heckled, spat at and hit with a placard. He didn't notice. He put out his hand and hailed a cab. Inside, with Perdita and Zel, he said to Zel, 'Can you tell me what is going on?'

They had taken the night flight. Xeno bought the tickets. On the plane as the lights went down it wasn't clear to Xeno whether he was flying through space or time. Time can't unhappen but it can be unlost. Can it?

★ ★ ★

Leo ran up the wide stairs to his offices. He was panting. Miss LaTrobe was standing there as though she had been born standing there.

'I did my best,' she said.

Perdita came into Reception. She ran to her father. 'Dad!'

'This man is your father?' said Leo. 'Xeno? Xeno?'

The two men stood staring at each other and Leo realised he was holding his hands so tight in a fist that his nails were cutting his palms. Not in anger. He could not speak now.

'Leo,' said Xeno.

They were like statues. Neither of them could move towards the other. The past was too strong.

There was a slamming sound downstairs. Pauline appeared in the office looking wild and unprepared. She saw Xeno and went straight for him, her arms round him, and he held her. 'I never thought I would see you again, Xeno. Never!'

Leo moved out of his trance. 'Can we go into my office?'

In the office Clo and Shep stood upright. Shep was carrying a cheap holdall. He unzipped it and took out the attaché case. Leo had never seen it, so he had no idea what was going on. Perdita spoke. 'Dad . . . '

Shep held up his hand. 'This is how the story started and this is where it starts again.'

Shep opened the case and took out the piece of sheet music. Pauline sat down on the white sofa like someone had pushed her. She tried to get up but some force made that impossible. Shep took out the faded velvet bag and poured the diamonds onto his broad palm.

'These are yours, Perdita. You know that.'

'Did you say Perdita?' said Leo. 'Her name's Miranda.'

'I'm Perdita,' said Perdita.

⋆ ⋆ ⋆

And the story fell out stone by stone, shining and held, the way time is held in a diamond, the way the light is held in each stone. And stones speak, and what was silent opens its mouth to tell a story and the story is set in stone to break the stone. What happened happened.

But.

The past is a grenade that explodes when thrown.

⋆ ⋆ ⋆

'Whose daughter is this?' said Leo. 'This Perdita? This Miranda?'

'Ours,' said Shep. 'She started out as yours and she became mine.'

Leo held out his hand for the necklace. Shep gave it to him.

'I recognised it,' said Xeno. 'Why did I not recognise it?'

Leo ran his fingers across the length of the necklace. 'I bought this for MiMi when we met.'

Shep said, 'The man you sent, Tony Gonzales, he put the baby in the BabyHatch of the Sainta Maria hospital for safe keeping. He was being followed for the money but I didn't know that then. We — Clo and me — tried to save him. Then I found Perdita.'

'So why didn't you take her to the police?'

'To be put in a children's home? To be adopted by strangers? I figured that anyone who could abandon his own child wasn't fit to be a father.'

'I didn't believe Perdita was my child,' said Leo. 'I thought she was Xeno's.'

'I knew she wasn't mine,' said Shep, 'but I loved her.'

'That's right!' said Clo.

'What did you do with the money?' said Leo.

'Leo!' Pauline had a particular tone and she had it now. Shep drew himself taller.

'I'm happy to answer, ma'am. That is why I am here. Leo, you're one of the guys who makes the world the way it is. I'm one of the guys who lives in the world the way it is. To you I'm a black man you see mostly doing Security or Delivery. And money and power being the most important things to you, you reckon they are the most important things to those who don't have them. Maybe to some people they are — because the way guys like you have fixed the world only a lottery ticket can change it for guys like me.

Hard work and hope won't do it any more. The American Dream is done.'

'I love our life,' said Perdita. 'What you made for us.'

'Perdita,' said Shep. 'The Fleece — I'm talking about our business back home, Leo — it's a piano bar where you get good music and good food. Perdita, the deeds to the place are fifty-fifty you and Clo. Because half was his mother's money — her life insurance when she died. And half is yours. None is mine.

'I guess we're different there, you and me, Leo, because owning doesn't mean that much to me. Seems like it's one of the miseries of the world.'

Leo was silent for longer than Leo was silent. Then he said, 'You steal my daughter and spend my cash and now you're in my office lecturing me on how to live?'

'Yes, I am,' said Shep.

Long pause. Pin drop. Breath held. Fingers crossed. Eyes closed. Can't look.

Pauline knew Leo better than anyone but she couldn't call what would happen next. Would he smash the moment into pieces or let it open into time?

Perdita went and stood by Shep and took his hand. Leo looked at her. He looked at all the years he hadn't had. At his refusal. And he saw his chance.

Leo held out his hand, stepping towards Shep.

'Thank you,' said Leo. 'I wish we'd met a long time ago.'

Shep took his hand.

Pauline tried to stand and flopped back. 'Who took my legs?'

And the tension broke and Clo high-fived Xeno, who looked like he needed a drink.

Suddenly Shep was exhausted. 'May I sit down? May I sit beside you . . . ?'

'Pauline,' said Pauline.

'I was just in hospital — a minor stroke. And we flew all night.'

And Shep collapsed his big body beside Pauline's small one and she took his hand.

'Where's your hotel?' said Leo.

'We don't even know what city we're in,' said Clo.

'I'll book you in at Claridge's, all of you — where's my PA?' Leo started yelling, 'VIRGINIA!'

Pauline said, 'Leo! They don't want to stay at Claridge's. This is our family. They can stay with me.'

'Anybody would think you were Jewish,' said Leo.

★ ★ ★

Xeno, Leo and Pauline took one cab. Shep and Clo and Perdita and Zel followed in another. Perdita sat beside her father just holding his hand.

Up ahead, Leo said to Pauline, 'Do you know where MiMi is?'

'You never asked me that before.'

'I was afraid you knew the answer.'

Pauline said, 'Time has been standing still for

293

eighteen years and now you want everything to happen at once.'

'I want MiMi to know about Perdita.'

The taxis pulled up outside the big brick house set back from the road.

'This is a fine house,' said Shep.

'This area used to be a dump,' said Pauline. 'Jews from the camps came here after the war. My grandparents had friends here — walk on the street, you could hear violins and accordians, mouth organs, mandolins. It was all music and all rooms for rent. This was a rooming house when I bought it — I had a tenant in the basement for ten years. She kept a donkey in the garden. Come in, come in.'

They went into the wide, welcoming hall with flowers on the table.

'Leo! Xeno! Go in the kitchen and make some tea! Zel! Clo! Can you bring the bags? I have six bedrooms and only one of them occupied as far as I know. I always thought I'd have a family, but you know that saying — build it and they will come? They didn't come.'

Shep went over to the grand piano in the bay window.

'This is a beautiful instrument. You play?'

'Since I was a girl,' said Pauline.

Shep was turning over the sheet music. 'You must be pretty good. Mozart. Beethoven. I'm self-taught. I can't play like this.'

'I can't play by ear,' said Pauline.

'Sure you can,' said Shep. 'I'll show you. May I?'

Shep sat at the piano. He started playing 'Summertime'. His big, confident hands were strong and beautiful. 'This piano has a wonderful tone.'

'What I paid for it,' said Pauline, 'it should be in Carnegie Hall.'

Perdita came and stood by him and began to sing. "Hush little baby, don't you cry . . . One of these mornings . . . "

Pauline sat down. The voice was as pure as MiMi's but had a deeper, more physical tone.

Leo and Xeno came out of the kitchen. Clo came in from the hall. 'That's my sister,' he said, his open face so proud.

Shep started to syncopate the melody on the piano, coming underneath, in and out of the top line, with his rich bass.

WAKE UP SINGING.

YOUR DADDY'S RICH.

YOUR MAMA'S GOOD-LOOKING.

★ ★ ★

Later that evening when everyone was eating round the big table in the kitchen, telling their stories, Pauline slipped out and booked the first morning train to Paris.

Xeno noticed her go. He stood up, hesitated, then went and helped himself to more chicken pie. Zel was filling up his own plate.

'Zel,' said Xeno, 'do you think we could talk?'

'What about?' said Zel, not looking at him.

'The fact that I have made a mess of life. That you are my son and I am proud of you.'

295

Zel didn't look at him. He went back to the table.

Xeno poured a glass of wine. Then he went to the sink, threw it away and took water from the fridge door.

★　★　★

Pauline was awake in her sleeping house at 4.30am and soon out of the door and into the empty streets to the corner where the taxi was waiting discreetly enough so that no one would know.

But Xeno knew she would go. He was in his room, padding barefoot to the window over the street, at the soft closing of the latch.

He opened his computer. In the game he looked up from the cold streets to MiMi's window, always dark. He had no wings that night.

In her window there was a light.

If This Be Magic . . .

Pauline took the Metro Line 4 to Cité.

She walked down the steps at Notre Dame and for an hour or so went back and forth between the ticket office for the tourist boats and the entrance to the Canal Saint-Martin.

The cobbled quay was busy. Men and women eating lunch. A party of schoolchildren bored with the history of the cathedral and waiting to catch a *vedette* to the Eiffel Tower. The dinner-and-dance boats closed and sleepy. The park keepers setting the sprinklers on the shrubby banks.

Is that her? They say it's her.

Pauline walked up to the small figure in the big coat, standing motionless watching the water. Pauline took out a simple A4 folder. Inside it was a handwritten piece of sheet music that said 'PERDITA' in stubby pencil.

★　★　★

And the world goes on regardless of joy or despair or one woman's fortune or one man's loss. And we can't know the lives of others. And we can't know our own lives beyond the details we can manage. And the things that change us forever happen without us knowing they would happen.

And the moment that looks like the rest is the

one where hearts are broken or healed. And time that runs so steady and sure runs wild outside of the clocks. It takes so little time to change a lifetime and it takes a lifetime to understand the change.

Music Wake Her

HollyPollyMolly were at the Roundhouse.

Leo was coping with his feelings by making everything around him as big and noisy and colourful as it could be so that he could pretend to himself he was in control.

'*Your girl-group called The Separations? Get them on a plane!*'

Perdita Skyped Holly and tried to explain and Shep phoned their father.

Leo was paying for their tickets but their father was adamant: his girls needed a chaperone.

'Who we gonna get?' said Clo. 'I don't trust any of my friends.'

'There's someone I can call,' said Shep. 'He came to visit me in hospital.'

'They'll have to share a room, Leo,' said Pauline. 'My house is full.'

'Pauline! This is a capital city of the world. There are hotels. Every unexpected visitor who lands at Heathrow doesn't have to stay at your house.'

'Like my house isn't good enough?'

Pauline had bought new clothes, lost weight, and she smiled a lot. 'You're happy, aren't you?' said Leo. 'You must be happy because you've stopped buying your clothes at Marks and Spencer.'

'Happy?' Pauline shrugged. 'Happy is too

303

goyisher, but I guess . . . I am . . . well, it's a kvell.'

'Do I ever know what you're talking about?' said Leo.

Then he said, 'What about MiMi?'

'There's an old Sephardi saying . . . '

'There would be . . . '

'Give time time.'

★ ★ ★

HollyPollyMolly were running through their numbers with Perdita and Shep when they heard someone clapping from the floor. The lights made it hard to see, but soon a familiar figure was waving at Shep.

It was Autolycus. 'Hey, Perdita! I hear you found your dad!'

'I never lost him. He's right there.'

'She's a good kid — I wish my kids were like her.'

'I didn't know you had any kids.'

'One story at a time or we'll be into *The Arabian Nights*.'

By now HollyPollyMolly were singing again and Pauline was coming towards the stage with a big carrier bag full of sandwiches.

'I am so hungry!' said Autolycus. 'Thank you, lady, thank you.'

He bit into a ham and cheese baguette.

'Who is this person?' said Pauline. 'Is he staying with me?'

★ ★ ★

304

Zel and Perdita were walking hand in hand through the hot evening. 'If you told this story to anyone they wouldn't believe it,' said Perdita. 'A month ago we were normal people.'

'They're the ones you've got to watch out for,' said Zel. 'I think it's all because of us.'

'What do you mean?'

'What I said before — in either life, the one they ruined, or this one, the one they couldn't ruin, because they couldn't find it — we were going to be together.'

'That's the Hollywood version.'

'Hollywood didn't invent fate.'

'So am I fated to spend the rest of my life with you?'

'No — that's where you get free will. You don't have to marry me.'

'Did you just ask me to marry you?'

Zel swung her in his arms like this is a happy ending.

★ ★ ★

Shep and Pauline were sitting in Pauline's garden. Pauline had told Shep the whole old story. When she got to the part about Tony Gonzales, Shep had his head in his hands. 'That's what he said! His last word:

'*Pauline*.

'Later I thought that must be the baby's name but we decided to call her Perdita because of the sheet music. It means little lost one, right?'

Pauline nodded. 'Tony said my name?'

'I swear it, Pauline. I always believed I'd done

the right thing. Now . . . I don't know any more.'

'You couldn't save Tony.'

'I tried, Pauline, believe me; we're not heroes, Clo and me, but we didn't cross to the other side of the road — we went in there.'

Pauline patted Shep's hand. 'Stop blaming yourself. You got nice hands, you know that? Tony had nice hands — working hands.'

Shep smiled at her and turned her hand over. 'You got giving hands — wide palms. But Pauline, if I had'a taken Perdita to the police she would'a been reunited with her mother.'

'And what kind of a childhood would it have been? The divorce, the horror of everything that happened afterwards. Milo. And Leo would have had Perdita half the time, MiMi the other half, and all the misery of loss and mistake and the two of them not able to speak to each other. Perdita is happy with you.'

'She never had a mother.'

'I don't know that MiMi could have been a mother to her. MiMi had a terrible breakdown. It wasn't only Perdita — it was Milo too.'

'Did you stay in touch with MiMi?'

She nodded. 'I have never told Leo. But he never asked either.'

'How did you forgive him?'

'He doesn't want to be forgiven. But how do you live if you don't forgive?'

Shep said, 'I think I was waiting for forgiveness from my wife — which was hard because she was dead. And because she was dead I was dead too — my heart was dead.

'When my wife died I couldn't remember how

306

to love — it was like she took the instructions with her. Then Perdita happened, like a miracle — it was a miracle — like a new start, the night, the rain, the moon like a planet coming in to land, and there she was, all wrapped in white like the moon had dressed her, and I tried to take her back, but I couldn't do it, because she was my instructions to love.'

Pauline put her other hand on Shep's. He covered her hand with his other hand. Pauline said, 'I love having you all in my house. I feel like I'll know you all forever. I've always lived here but I feel like I've come home.'

Shep said, 'You ever been to Louisiana?'

At that moment the back door opened and Autolycus came out into the garden. He waved. 'Just off to my shepherd's hut. Nice place you got here, Pauline. Do you play poker?'

⋆ ⋆ ⋆

Shep and Pauline went inside. Shep sat down at the piano and started improvising. Pauline came and sat by him. 'I wish I could do that.'

'Here . . . I'll play the left hand and you put in some tunes to my chords.'

They started to do that. Pauline was hesitant — laughing. 'How do you do those great big chords?'

'That is Pentecostal piano. I guess there are no Jewish Pentecostals?'

'Maybe I just haven't met them yet.'

'These are chords for the Second Coming.'

'That'll be my problem, then — we're still

waiting for the Messiah on his first visit.'

Pauline spread her hands — she was fast and deft and she could pick out a tune when Shep was guiding her with the chords.

'That's it! You're getting it now! I'll book you a guest residency at the Fleece. You can earn your keep. Now try the left hand too — just stay in key and do these blockbuster chords. I'll come behind you.'

Shep stood behind Pauline, leaning over her, his long arms on either side, guiding her hands and putting in a little jazz. He leaned in closer. Pauline leaned back against him. He put his arms round her.

It was the day of the concert.

★ ★ ★

Perdita was nervous because the girls hadn't been able to rehearse the day before — the building was closed for the get-in and the tech. She and Zel had walked by the Roundhouse late at night on their way back to Pauline's. The lights were all on and the band was playing.

'That's weird,' said Perdita. 'Sounds like a rehearsal.'

They tried the big front doors and the stage door but the place was locked up.

When they got back they mentioned it to Pauline, who was on her way out. 'Just a technical problem,' she said. 'I'm just going down there myself.'

'It's midnight,' said Perdita.

'I'm a pumpkin already,' said Pauline. 'No worries.'

★ ★ ★

It was the day of the concert.

'I have some bad news for you, Leo,' said Pauline.

'I don't care,' said Leo. 'How much have we lost?'

'You don't care?'

'It's just business. Look what we found. We found Perdita.'

'The Secretary of State has called in the planning permission for the Roundhouse.'

'We've been granted planning permission.'

'Our major backer has been charged with bribery, corruption and conspiring to pervert the course of justice.'

Leo looked relieved. 'That's fine. It will take five years and a team of lawyers and he'll get off. What's the problem?'

'He's confessed.'

'Oshitavitch has confessed?'

'Plea bargaining. I think there were a couple of murders too.'

'Murders? Why didn't you say? That's more difficult. What's it mean for us?'

'The long version is we fight it. The short version is you don't knock it down.'

'I've been trying to knock down the Roundhouse since . . . '

'MiMi sang here.'

'OK, so it's personal.'

'Leo, life is personal. You held it at arm's length until it came too close and then you killed it.'

'Pauline?'

Leo sat down on the floor, his back against the wall. A man not young. A boy who had never grown up. He was sobbing. Pauline knelt down in front of him.

'I've thought of killing myself so many times. I don't do it, not because I am a coward, but because it would be easier for me to be dead. What's my life? I make money and I have memories. That's not a life. I don't kill myself because living is my own life sentence. I don't want your pity, Pauline. I just want you to know.'

'I do know,' said Pauline. 'That's why I'm still here.'

★　★　★

It was the night of the concert.

Pauline had had her hair done. She'd been to Elaine in Golders Green. 'I want big hair, Elaine. Special occasion.'

Elaine stood Pauline's hair on end like she had seen one of those ghosts nobody sees.

'There's enough length — some spray, some hold. You want me to schlepp it up?'

'Schlepp it up, Elaine.'

★　★　★

Autolycus was freshly minted in a Camden Town suit. 'You look the cut, Toly,' said Pauline.

'Only my mother ever called me Toly,' said Autolycus. 'I could fix you up with a nice car if you come out west. Do you make chicken soup, by any chance?'

'What do you think?' said Pauline. 'Toly, I just want to ask you. Zel . . . is he a good boy — I know he's not a Jew but is he a good boy?'

'Never let him hear me say this,' said Autolycus, 'it would compromise my authority. He's the best. That boy's the best. Sure, he's had

311

a good teacher . . . '

★ ★ ★

Xeno was standing outside Pauline's house.

Zel came out wearing a black suit and a white T-shirt. Xeno was wearing black jeans, black T-shirt and pink suede shoes.

'You are so gay,' said Zel.

'We were the style industry before you were born,' said Xeno. 'Nice suit.'

Zel hesitated. Then he smiled. Xeno hesitated. Then he smiled. 'I'd like to get to know you.'

Zel hesitated. 'I guess I'm walking down there. You walking too?'

★ ★ ★

Clo had never met a woman the same height as him.

'When did you first read Hemingway?' said Lorraine LaTrobe.

Clo couldn't say he had never read Hemingway. That the book had stayed in his jacket long after Autolycus had given it to him. That the jacket and the book had come to London and that Clo had left his jacket in Leo's office and Lorraine LaTrobe had picked up the book as it fell out when she picked up the jacket.

She was pretty sexy.

'*The Sun Also Rises* is my favourite Hemingway,' said Lorraine LaTrobe, 'but I love *A Moveable Feast* too. The memoir. His time in Paris — Shakespeare and Company.'

312

'Yeah, right,' said Clo. 'That bookstore.'

Lorraine LaTrobe ran one powerful hand down the inside of Clo's powerful thigh.

★ ★ ★

HollyPollyMolly were backstage getting into their new dresses.

Perdita was still in the shower. She felt nervous and unfocused. It wasn't like her.

Shep knocked on the door. Perdita answered it in her dressing gown with her hair in a towel. 'Hi, Dad.'

Shep came in. 'You OK? What is it?'

Everything, but she couldn't say it. Too much, but she couldn't explain it. Enough, but she couldn't understand why what she wanted seemed to have happened and she didn't want it at all. She felt like Eve after the apple.

'It's Friday; we should be at the bar serving clams and asking people to choose a song.'

'We can go home soon.'

But we can't, she thought, *because home isn't where we left it. If I could wind back time, I would.*

But Shep knew her thoughts.

'We can't go back to where we were, or who we were, that's true. But we can still go home.'

He gave her a hug.

There was a knock at the door. It was Clo and Lorraine LaTrobe. 'We've come to wish you luck, little sister,' said Clo. Lorraine LaTrobe was dressed in a skintight one-piece Lycra suit and spike heels. Her hair was piled on her head and dyed red like a stop light.

'You look amazing,' said Perdita. 'Are you on your bike?'

'I don't have a bike. Bikes are for vegans.'

She put her arm round Clo. He looked sheepish. 'Hi, Dad.'

Pauline came down the corridor with her hair in a towel. 'It's time! Hi, Lorraine.'

'Hello, Mrs Levy,' said Lorraine. 'We'll be in the front row.'

She took Clo's hand and led him off.

'She's quite a woman,' said Shep.

'She's trans,' said Pauline.

'Trans what?' said Shep.

'Don't worry about it, Dad,' said Perdita.

'So are you ready?' said Shep. 'It's time.'

It was the night of the concert.

The big space was full. Red lanterns and red lights lit the audience. The raised stage was silver-white with a big grand piano and drum kit and plenty of room for the brass section. There were a couple of local breaking bands, two performance poets, a stand-up comedian and a fire eater.

★　★　★

The Separations finished their set. The audience loved them. 'I could sell them,' said Leo. Pauline pulled her *oy vey* face at him. 'Don't you know the old saying: don't boil your children to make into spoons?'

'Can you cut the Yidderish and tell me what's happening?' said Leo. 'Why are they rearranging the stage? Who are those guys coming on to play?'

'That's her band.' Said Pauline.

'Whose band?' Said Leo.

The theatre and the stage went black. Blackout-black like a night in a dream. And then there was a light, high up like a light in a window. And were those feathers falling from the rig, or was it snow? And were there diamonds mixed in with the snow and the feathers, shining like another chance?

315

And the follow-spot lit up an empty space that had been empty for as long as anyone could remember, and what is memory but a rope slung across time?

★ ★ ★

A woman is standing like a statue in the light. She's wearing a simple black dress and red lipstick, her heavy hair cut short.

She doesn't move. Then she does.

'This song is for my daughter. It's called 'Perdita'.'

★ ★ ★

Leo stood up, went into the aisle. From somewhere in the theatre Xeno came and stood beside him. He put his arm round Leo. Leo was crying now, long tears of rain.

That which is lost is found.

★ ★ ★

So we leave them now, in the theatre, with the music. I was sitting at the back, waiting to see what would happen, and now I'm out on the street in the summer night, the rain tracing my face.

★ ★ ★

I wrote this cover version because the play has been a private text for me for more than thirty years. By that I mean part of the written wor(l)d

I can't live without; without, not in the sense of lack, but in the old sense of living outside of something.

It's a play about a foundling. And I am. It's a play about forgiveness and a world of possible futures — and how forgiveness and the future are tied together in both directions. Time is reversible.

★ ★ ★

The late plays of Shakespeare depend on forgiveness.

But what is it that's forgiven?

The Winter's Tale revisits *Othello*. A man who would rather murder the world than change himself. But this time the heroine doesn't have to die in the service of the hero's delusions. It is really himself that Othello can't love or trust — not Desdemona — but when Shakespeare returns to this theme, he brings with him a second chance.

Hermione doesn't die. And Leontes and Polixenes don't die either. And the future is secured because Florizel and Perdita won't behave like their fathers. Will they?

Forgiveness. There are only three possible endings to a story — if you put aside And They All Lived Happily Ever After, which isn't an ending, but a coda.

The three possible endings are:

Revenge. Tragedy. Forgiveness.

Shakespeare knew all about revenge and tragedy.

Towards the end of his working life he became interested in forgiveness — or rather, he became interested again in forgiveness — because it's there in the character of Helena against the selfish, spoilt Bertram's pornographic narcissism in *All's Well That Ends Well*, and it's there in Isabella against the lustful savagery of *Measure for Measure*. And it's there in Portia, the poet of mercy against the killing debt of a pound of flesh. It's not that Shylock is a Jew — it's that he's not enough of a Jew. The Old Testament is predicated on wiping the slate clean: forgiving the debt. The past must not mortgage the future.

Supremely, forgiveness is the measure of Cordelia and Hermione. In *King Lear*, Cordelia dies in the service of love, battling another pair of Shakespeare's Hostile Brothers, Edmund and Edgar (think how often he uses that device — and what else are Leontes and Polixenes?). Cordelia is caught too between her sisters, Goneril and Regan, serpents as deadly as Lady Macbeth, in thrall, like her, to the power-plays of maleness. Lear, as a father, does not protect his youngest child from his own madness, just as Leontes abandons Perdita to kites and ravens, wolves and bears. Shakespeare was not an enthusiast of family life; would you want to be raised by a Montague or a Capulet? Would you want parents like Hamlet's parents?

Miranda, in Shakespeare's final play, *The Tempest*, gets a father worth being born for — but there are only the two of them on the island, and when Ferdinand appears, Prospero teeters on the edge of the usual jealous rage, proofing himself against the future by refusing to let it happen. He doesn't give in to the rage — and Shakespeare walks away from the play, as we do, leaving it to the kids to get it right next time.

As Ezra Pound said, 'Make it new.'

★   ★   ★

The Winter's Tale is a play where the past depends on the future just as much as the future depends on the past. The past in *The Winter's Tale* is not history; it's tragedy. And tragedy can't happen without consciousness. It is the scale of the loss, the sense of it and its senselessness, that makes the jealousy and violence of the first act so painful.

Part Two, with its dancing shepherds and easy pastoral, is an obvious contrast to the dark, shadowed halls of Sicilia. The values of the Shepherd and his son, the Clown, are right-minded virtues compared to the self-justifying sophistries of metropolitan minds.

Polixenes, who has had our sympathy in Act One, proves himself as conventional and irrational as Leontes, when in Part Two he tries to wreck the love between his son, Florizel, and Perdita with death threats as sexually sadistic as anything dreamed up by Leontes.

Perdita is too common for his boy. It's a misreading of the female as fatal as Leontes's misreading of Hermione or Lear's misreading of Cordelia.

That everything comes right in Part Three

looks like a sleight of hand but it isn't. Leontes's repentance is real. He has hated himself for 16 years. Hermione's steadfastness is the opposite of the hasty violence of Leontes in Act One or the cruel rage of Polixenes in Part Two.

Hermione does the thing most difficult to do to right a wrong situation: nothing.

Nothing is the key word of the play. Leontes's demented speech on the supposed adultery contains its own answer, but he can't hear it:

> Is whispering nothing?
> Is leaning cheek to cheek? Is meeting noses?
> Kissing with inside lip? Stopping the career
> Of laughter with a sigh? — a note infallible
> Of breaking honesty. Horsing foot on foot?
> Skulking in corners? Wishing clocks more
>   swift,
> Hours minutes, noon midnight? And all
>   eyes
> Blind with the pin and web but theirs,
>   theirs only,
> That would unseen be wicked? Is this
>   nothing?
> Why then the world and all that's in't is
>   nothing,
> The covering sky is nothing, Bohemia
>   nothing,
> My wife is nothing, nor nothing have these
>   nothings
> If this be nothing.

After the nuclear wastes of Leontes's fallout, there is nothing that can be done until the next generation is ready to remedy it — and they too must first escape the necrotic longings of the past, as Perdita avoids death for a second time.

This is an 'old tale', a fairy tale. But in a fairy tale the threat usually comes from the outside — a dragon or an army or an evil sorcerer. Shakespeare, anticipating Freud, puts the threat where it really is: on the inside.

The Winter's Tale was first performed in 1611. It took another three hundred years before the nascent science of psychoanalysis began to understand how the past mortgages the future, or that the past can be redeemed. How the past lies in wait as an ambush, or as a beggar in disguise. Shakespeare loved disguises; one thing or one kind masquerading as another — a girl who's a boy who's a girl. A princess who is a shepherdess who is a goddess. A statue that comes to life. That things are not what they seem is the terror and the glory of *The Winter's Tale*.

And time, that sets all limits, offers our one chance at freedom from limits. We were not trapped after all. Time can be redeemed. That which is lost is found . . .

So let the last word be hers.

PERDITA

Soon this will become our life together and we have to live in the world like everyone else. We have to go to work, have children, make homes, make dinner, make love and the world is low on goodness these days so our lives may come to nothing. We will have dreams but will they come true?

Maybe we'll forget that we were the site where the miracle happened. The place of pilgrimage that fell into disuse, overgrown with weeds, run-down and neglected. Maybe we won't stay together. Maybe life is too hard anyway. Maybe love is just for the movies.

Maybe we'll hurt each other so much that we will deny that what happened happened. We'll find an alibi to prove that we were never there. Those people didn't exist.

Maybe, one night, when the weather is bad and you are holding my wrists too tight, I'll take a torch and go for a walk in the rain, my collar up against the wind, and the stars not there in the dark, and a bird startles out of the hedge, and there's the gleam of puddles under battery-light, and further off the sound of the main road, but here the sound of the night and my footsteps and my breathing.

Maybe then I will remember that, although history repeats itself and we always fall, and I am a carrier of history whose brief excursion into time leaves no mark, I have known something worth knowing, wild and unlikely and against every rote.

Like a pocket of air in an upturned boat.

Love. The size of it. The scale of it. Unimaginable. Vast. Your love for me. My love for you. Our love for one another. Real. Yes. Though I find my way by flashlight in the dark, I am witness and evidence of what I know: this love.

The atom and jot of my span.

Acknowledgements

And thanks to: my agent and my friend, Caroline Michel. The team at Chatto, especially Juliet Brooke and Becky Hardie. Rachel Cugnoni and Áine Mulkeen at Vintage. My colleagues at the University of Manchester, especially John McAuliffe. Laura Evans who managed the copyedit and my mad proofs, and Val McDermid who solved a problem. And to Susie Orbach — who married me.

And last but not least: to William Shakespeare. Wherever you are.

HOGARTH
SHAKESPEARE

'He was not of an age, but for all time'
Ben Jonson

For more than four hundred years Shakespeare's works have been performed, read and loved throughout the world. They have been reinterpreted for each new generation, whether as teen films, musicals, science-fiction flicks, Japanese warrior tales or literary transformations.

The Hogarth Press was originally founded by Virginia and Leonard Woolf in 1917, with a mission to publish the best new writing of the age. The Hogarth Shakespeare sees Shakespeare's works retold by acclaimed and bestselling novelists of today. The series launched in October 2015 in over twenty countries. It promises to excite imaginations all around the world.

Margaret Atwood, *The Tempest*
Tracy Chevalier, *Othello*
Gillian Flynn, *Hamlet*
Howard Jacobson, *The Merchant of Venice*
Jo Nesbø, *Macbeth*
Edward St Aubyn, *King Lear*
Anne Tyler, *The Taming of the Shrew*
Jeanette Winterson, *The Winter's Tale*

We do hope that you have enjoyed reading this large print book.

Did you know that all of our titles are available for purchase?

We publish a wide range of high quality large print books including:
Romances, Mysteries, Classics
General Fiction
Non Fiction and Westerns

Special interest titles available in large print are:
The Little Oxford Dictionary
Music Book
Song Book
Hymn Book
Service Book

Also available from us courtesy of Oxford University Press:
Young Readers' Dictionary
(large print edition)
Young Readers' Thesaurus
(large print edition)

For further information or a free brochure, please contact us at:
Ulverscroft Large Print Books Ltd.,
The Green, Bradgate Road, Anstey,
Leicester, LE7 7FU, England.
Tel: (00 44) 0116 236 4325
Fax: (00 44) 0116 234 0205